THE THEORY OF 21

FOR THE 21ST CENTURY

CHUCK REAVES, CSP. CPAE

The Theory of 21 by Chuck Reaves
©2005 by Chuck Reaves
All Rights Reserved

ISBN: 1-59755-018-3

Published by: ADVANTAGE BOOKS™

www.advbooks.com

This book and parts thereof may not be reproduced in any form, stored in a retrieval system or transmitted in any form by any means (electronic, mechanical, photocopy, recording or otherwise) without prior written permission of the author, except as provided by United States of America copyright law.

Library of Congress Control Number: 2005931510

Twenty One Associates Press
P.O. Box 13447
Atlanta, GA 30324
770 979-3321

First Printing: August 2005

08 09 10 11 12 01 02   9 8 7 6 5 4 3 2 1

Printed in the United States of America

TABLE OF CONTENTS

Introduction v

Chapter 1: The Theory of 21 ....…................   1

Chapter 2: The Quest for A Yes 17

Chapter 3: The Negative Twenty (-20) 43

Chapter 4: The Positive Twenty (+20) ....….................. 73

Chapter 5: The 21's 105

Chapter 6: Building 21's 143

Chapter 7: Types of 21's 169

Chapter 8: Spiritual Transformation 197

The Theory of 21 Test 201

Chuck Reaves

Introduction

The Theory of 21

In the late 1960's, a young soldier returned from Vietnam and went to look for a job. He learned quickly that the medals on his chest and the year of combat experience were seemingly of little value to corporate America.

Lacking a college degree or any meaningful skills, he accepted an offer from AT&T to an entry-level position where he would spend the next ten years soldering wires. Every morning for ten years he would wake up, put on his blue jeans and go down to the phone company and solder wires for eight or sixteen hours a day.

All he ever did was solder wires because all he ever thought he was capable of doing was soldering wires. His had been a life where there had been few successes and plenty of people telling him that he would never amount to anything. He was accustomed to living down to others' expectations of him.

After a series of calamities, he found himself reevaluating his life. At the same time, a senior manager at AT&T saw something in the thirty-something man and offered to put him in sales. He declined the offer even though it could have meant a substantial improvement in his lifestyle. His reasons were that he was under-educated, too shy and timid, lacked interpersonal skills and did not own a suit.

The manager, Lem Anderson, leaned across his desk, looked me in the eye and said, "I want you to try it for me."

In the next five years I would enjoy seven promotions at AT&T. In my first full year as an Account Executive I was named the top salesperson out of 1,100 salespeople. In the Atlanta sales office, I was the only salesperson without a college degree and one of only a few who did not have an MBA.

How had this happened?

I had good people who gave me good advice and good help all along the way. This book will help you find the people who will help you.

As you might imagine, all along the way there were people who were giving me all of the reasons why I could not succeed in sales. Some implied it with statements like, "Hey, that's pretty good, just settle for that. I will take it from here."

Some were more overt. One salesperson in Birmingham made a special effort to call me and tell me that, "Those of us with a college degree have a lot more on the ball than people who don't."

How did a timid, insecure, undereducated person find himself on the top of the heap? The answer was, simply, persistence. I never gave up.

It took me a long time to realize that 90% of success is just showing up and another 9.9% is just staying there. This was not an intentional process for me nor was it a part of something I had been taught. Like most good ideas, it came out of ignorance. Let me explain.

When I went to work for AT&T in an entry-level position, I had just completed two years of service in the military. In the armed forces, when someone tells you to do something, what do you do? You do

Introduction: The Theory of 21

it! In an entry-level position in a major corporation, when someone tells you to do something, what do you do? You do it.

Two years in the military and ten years in an entry-level job had combined into twelve years of conditioned behavior. People would tell me to do something and I would do it.

When I went into sales, my manager told me to go sell certain products to certain people. What did I think I was supposed to do? Sell those products to those people. I did not know there were any options; I assumed I had to sell.

At that time, AT&T had the highest prices, the oldest technology and longest delivery intervals. Other than that we were pretty competitive. I would make my sales call just like they taught me in sales school. Unlike the role-playing instructors in sales school, however, the customers would turn me down. They would send me out of their offices. They would occasionally refuse to see me.

What was I to do? I had to sell to these people – my boss said so.

I kept going back. I would take a different approach each time, never going back with the same presentation twice. I don't know if they felt sorry for me or got tired of seeing me but enough of them bought from me to make the top producer.

I was promoted to sales manager and assumed the leadership of a sales team. On my first day I called a meeting and asked for questions. Every Account Executive in the room had the same question: "You were top salesperson last year, I want to be the top salesperson this year, how did you do it?"

My answers were not good enough for them. "Do what they taught us in sales school," and, "Learn the products' features and benefits," were unacceptable answers. They said they were already doing those things and wanted to know what I was doing differently.

After more than an hour we finally hit upon the difference in my selling style and theirs. I kept going back to see the customers even when they said no.

So, my teammates asked me how many times they should go back. I had no idea; I had never thought about it. So I picked a number out of the air and said twelve. Then I told them that if they would try to sell a product, service, application or project to a customer and the customer still refused to buy after twelve attempts, I would take that objective out of their quota.

I was not really allowed to do that, so what I had decided was that if they did not sell it, I would put the objective into my MBO's (remember them?) and take responsibility for the sale.

No Account Executive ever brought me a failed sale.

After a few attempts the AE's found a way to sell the customer. They uncovered hidden objectives. They found new ways to quantify their solution. Sales became fun again for most of them because they were now hanging in until their success became a reality.

After leaving AT&T to become a speaker, I began speaking on the topic of persistence. I use 21 now instead of twelve and the principle is the same. So are the results.

Since first releasing the concept I have heard from hundreds of people directly and thousands indirectly about how this concept improved their lives.

Introduction: The Theory of 21

You are invited to join the other winners who are living their dreams by following the concepts in this book.

You will find some valuable ideas and some helpful reminders this book. Yes, some of it you have heard before; some will be new. Whenever possible, I have used stories to illustrate some of the important concepts. You may want to use these stories in some way so I have changed the font and highlighted the subject of each story to make it easier for you to find them.

Once you have an understanding of the concepts in this book, Teach Others!

Chuck Reaves

Chapter One

The Theory of 21

What is the secret to success?

My desire to answer that question led to a quest of some nine years. I interviewed hundreds of successful people. These were people whose pictures had appeared on magazine covers and who had written best selling books. They were also the founders of businesses you may never hear about but companies employing hundreds of workers. Some of the people are world renowned, others are virtual unknowns outside of their area of expertise.

Sometimes I would call these people and be transferred to an assistant or be sent a copy of something the person had written. No matter, I got the answer to my question, "What is your secret to success?"

I read scores of biographies and autobiographies. After all, I could not interview Thomas Edison or Harvey Firestone.

As a result of all of this research, there was only one trait that all of these successful people had in common. In three words it is: "Never Give Up". In two words it is "Try Again". In a single word it is "Persistence". Persistence is the foundation for the Theory of 21.

> **There is a lot more to persistence than simply not quitting**

If that sounds simplistic, it is. There is a lot more to persistence than simply not quitting. (After all, there are quite a few pages left in this book, so there must be more to it than just not quitting.) I had to learn the ins and outs of trying over and over again. That is what this book is about: how you can use persistence to achieve whatever goal or goals you want to accomplish. It is also about finding those people who can help you in attaining your goals.

Successful people come from every type of background imaginable. Some were raised in affluent homes; others came from the wrong side of the tracks. Some were very well educated; others were virtually illiterate. There was not even a commonality in their attitudes - there were die hard *pessimists* in the lot. The only thing they had in common was that they never gave up.

Some succeeded in business, others in the arts. Many were famous for their accomplishments in athletics, others served, and continue to serve as an inspiration to us simply because they can walk when the medical profession had sentenced them to life in a wheelchair. Some succeeded in curing illnesses and bringing about peace in war ravaged areas, others were successful in accomplishing seemingly lesser objectives.

What would you like to accomplish? Do you want to write a great symphony or do you want to learn how to play the piano? The same principles apply to both. There will be just as many people telling you that you are too old, lazy, tone deaf or untalented to learn how to play the piano as there are people using the same arguments for you're never attaining the goal of writing an entire symphony.

> **You will have many opportunities to quit. Don't.**

Interesting, isn't it? Whether great or small, your goal will meet resistance from many people and assistance from a few. There will be many opportunities to quit and plenty of people encouraging you

Chapter One: The Theory of 21

to throw in the towel. However, there will be those special few who will not only encourage you; they will help make a way for your dream to become a reality.

Every successful person has had at least one significant opportunity to quit, and they didn't take it. There was the time when they could have thrown in the towel and no one would have blamed them. In fact, many of their so-called friends were actually encouraging them to quit. (When you have completed this book, you will understand why.)

There is a right way and a wrong way to persist. There are people who will help you, the ones I call the 21's. There are people who will stand in your way, the Negative Twenties (*-20's*) and there are people who will appear to be helping who are actually doing everything in their power to cause you to give up, the Positive Twenties (*+20's*). Being able to discern who is really helping you and who is actually trying to stop or divert you will be critical to your success.

Again, there is a right way and a wrong way to persist. For example, I once sat on the beach and watched a young child dig a hole in the sand. Then he took his bucket to the ocean, filled it and emptied it in the hole. The sand immediately absorbed the water. He went back to the ocean for another bucketful and emptied it into the hole with the same results. This went on for probably ten minutes. Finally a man who appeared to be the kid's father gave him the sad news. "You'll never be able to fill the hole with water, son." "I'm not trying to fill the hole", the kid replied, "I'm emptying the ocean".

Believe it or not, there are adults with the same misguided objectives. We're too smart to try to empty the ocean with a pail, but we can be making the same fundamental error if we are not careful. There are goals that are unattainable. There are laws of physics and other factors that rule over any amount of positive thinking. Before you continue in this book and learn to be more persistent in achieving your goals, test them against the foundations for good ideas that follow in this introduction.

I opened a fortune cookie a couple of years ago that said, "You will win the Miss America title". Being married, male and over fifty makes that prediction highly unlikely. I could pursue changing the rules of the pageant, claiming that the current rules discriminate against males, married people and folks over thirty. I could probably find an attorney to take the case all the way to the Supreme Court if I wanted to spend my money that way.

But why should I? On the one hand, achieving an honor like being Miss America could give me the introductions and power to accomplish great things. On the other hand, my success in achieving that honor would actually be diluted by knowing that I had achieved my objective at the expense of significantly altering what the Miss America title represents. Besides, there are other ways I could achieve the same benefits, aren't there?

> **I could become the next Miss America – but why?**

So we must regularly reevaluate our goals by asking ourselves if the goal we set in the past is still viable based on what we have learned in the meantime. I regularly review my goals and make sure the set goal is the still the best method for meeting my objectives.

There is an even more basic question here: Who *really* set the goal? Did I establish the goal based on something *I* wanted to do? Or, was the goal based on what an outsider said I should do? Who is setting your goals for you?

How could the same time, energy and resources be used to accomplish something more worthwhile and of greater lasting value?

Chapter One: The Theory of 21

There are some basic standards an idea has to meet in order to be a good idea. These standards can be verified using the following questions. To help you verify that you are seeking a worthwhile goal, write out your goal and then answer these questions.

What would happen if I succeeded?

The kid with the sand bucket at the beach has not thought his plan through, nor does he have the knowledge to do so. He does not understand things like ecological balance, the actual size of the ocean or the basic laws of physics. In other words, he lacks fundamental knowledge. What about your goal? What would really happen if you achieved your goal? Have you asked the right people the right questions?

> **...he lacked fundamental knowledge**

We occasionally hear movie stars and famous musicians lamenting that they cannot go out in public because so many people speak to them and want autographs. Hey, if you're going to have a problem, have *that* one! What is the real story here? Are these people on a whining pity party? Or, did they not think through what having the success would mean?

If I fought the battles and became the recipient of the title now known as Miss America, what would I have earned? I would have the satisfaction of knowing I had succeeded in changing an established and respected pageant into something more like what I wanted it to be. But what is the real accomplishment worth? Would people jeer at me in public? Would I receive hate mail? Would I be ridiculed in the press?

To understand this, think about Shannon Faulkner, the first woman admitted to the Citadel. She accomplished the previously impossible goal of entering a formerly all male institution. Once there, the physical, mental and emotional rigors took their toll and she washed out in three days. Many other first year cadets also washed out. But because she had made such an issue of being allowed entry and because she had upset someone else's domain, she was subjected to ridicule, jeers in public, hate mail, bad press, etc.

This is a key question: **Are you ready to <u>have</u> your dream or is the real goal just <u>achieving</u> the dream?**

> *A few years ago several prisoners in a North Carolina prison planned and executed an incredible escape. Through detailed choreography and with precise timing, the prisoners managed to overpower several guards whose uniforms fit them perfectly. Then the escaping men took possession of a state truck at precisely the right time and drove out of the prison gates, waving casually to the guards at the gate as they left. They had accomplished their dream, their goal, or had they?*
>
> *Within two days most of the escaped prisoners were back in custody. Three of them had been captured only a few miles from where the daring escape had occurred. They were sitting in a Laundromat drinking wine and eating cheese. They had a plan to <u>become</u> free men; they had no plan to <u>be</u> free men.*

Some other questions you want to ask are, **"How would my life change for the better?"**, as well as, **"How would my life change for the worse?"**, if my goal were attained.

Chapter One: The Theory of 21

> Based on <u>your</u> definition of success, are you setting yourself up for success or failure?

The 21 thinks this through and anticipates a positive outcome. The *20's* only consider the negatives - what could go wrong.

> *How would my success affect others?*

It is one thing for you to set a goal to have a Cadillac like your neighbor's. It is something else for you to set a goal to have your neighbor's Cadillac. The Cadillac car company can make as many cars as people are willing to buy so we do not need to rob someone else of theirs. There is no shortage of Cadillacs.

> ***THERE IS NO SHORTAGE OF SUCCESS IN THIS WORLD. THERE IS ONLY A SHORTAGE OF PEOPLE WITH THE WILL TO PURSUE IT***

Similarly, there is no shortage of success in this world. There is only a shortage of people with the will to pursue it. No one has to suffer or relinquish anything for you to have whatever you want.

If one person's goals or success precludes someone else's success or goals, it probably won't happen. The reason is that goal setters pursue their dreams. If two people are going for the exact same thing, a lot of energy will be wasted while both parties ignore the other possibilities.

For instance, two men have their eyes on the same woman. Both men decide that their success is predicated on marrying this woman, and only this woman. No other person could possibly replace this individual. Thinking this way ignores other possibilities. Is it this woman or the traits she possess that is attractive to each man? If it is the traits, who are the other women who also possess these traits? If it is her sphere of influence, who else has the same level of influence? Most importantly, this attitude ignores one very significant possibility: the woman has a mind of her own. Maybe *she* will determine which, if either, man is most suitable for *her* success.

Whenever others are involved, the goal must be a win - win. Otherwise it will be a lose - lose. There is no middle ground. This point will be proven many times over throughout this book, as will another point: 21's help other 21's win. They even attempt to help *20's* win occasionally. *20's* see only the win - lose or lose - lose possibilities.

> **21's help other 21's win**

Is attaining this goal good for me?

Good can mean healthy, wise or even safe.

If we set a goal to attain something that is unhealthy, our own minds will work against us. God has built some safeguards into us. If we touch something hot, like a flame, our reflexes take over and cause us to jerk our hand out of harm's way. Fighting natural reflexes is difficult and can be impossible. So, if we set a goal that will ultimately prove to be unhealthy, our inner self will fight it.

This is not to say that we cannot set goals that are contrary to our learned behavior. In fact, most significant goals are by design contrary to our learned behavior. If they weren't, they would already be a part of us, wouldn't they? If losing weight were a natural part of our behavior, no one would ever set a goal to lose weight. Yet, weight loss and getting in shape are the two most common goals people set.

Chapter One: The Theory of 21

If a goal is unwise it is likewise subject to failure. The reason for this is that we all need others to help us attain our goals. "I get by with a little help from my friends". To garner their cooperation, we have to sell our mentors or friends on the goal. It is hard to sell foolishness. In fact, the type of person who is most likely to help us attain our goal is also the type of person who will resent being asked to assist in doing something unwise.

For instance, can you imagine asking Billy Graham to help you plan a bank robbery? If you could spend time with him and you asked him how you could feed ten thousand starving people in a third world country, he would brainstorm with you and encourage you. But if you were planning something unwise, he would terminate the conversation.

We cannot set goals that are dangerous. Whether the goal risks life and limb or the safety of our business, our minds will not work on our behalf to attain a dangerous goal. We have all seen the movies where the action hero inflicts pain on himself to attain some goal. When we see that on the screen, it's Hollywood. When we see it in real life, it's a sign of weakness. Our minds do not normally or naturally support our endeavors to harm ourselves.

> **Real success goals may be high risk, but they are not *dangerous***

So, for persistence to be a part of our process for our success, our definition of success must be smart. It must also be wise. None of the successful people I studied kept on doing things that were not working. It is unwise to think that doing something over and over and getting the wrong results will suddenly bring the right results if we just do it often enough.

21's know what they want and they seek alternatives to make it happen. *20's* know what they want to prevent from happening and they use rote, tried-and-true responses to achieve their objective.

> *By the time he was thirty-six years old he had already failed at four businesses. One night he was working late, as usual, and he went to his ledger to close out the day's business. The bottom line must not have been what he expected because he wrote across the page, "I have worked two years for nothing. Damn. Damn. Damn. Damn." A short time later, this business also failed.*

> *In 1858 he went to New York and tried again. This time he tried a new philosophy since the previous ones had not brought about the desired results. He was a retailer and had always tried to sell the more expensive products, an area where he lacked expertise or experience. This time he would concentrate on lower priced items, sell them at the lowest possible prices and sell for cash only.*

> *He opened his doors and on his first day of business he took in only $11.06.*

> *His name was Rowland Macy, or R.H. Macy. His store not only thrived, it became an institution and a landmark in New York. (And you thought discount stores were a new phenomena.)*

Over the years Macy learned how to sell the upper end products as well as the lower priced items. This led to the popularity of department stores, stores with numerous different sections, each offering different categories of merchandise and multiple price points.

Chapter One: The Theory of 21

The secret to Macy's success begins with the fist pounding frustration that acknowledges that what we are doing isn't working. The next step is to find another way to accomplish what we want to accomplish. Remember, Macy had already failed five times. He knew he could be a merchant. He wanted it, he believed in it, he just needed another procedure to make it work.

> ***Finding an alternative way of doing something is a two-step process.***

Step One, identify the source of the frustration. What is causing you to feel stymied or diverted? When Macy was failing, he stopped, took stock of himself and his accomplishments and learned that he had been concentrating on selling the wrong products. He knew ordinary products and their buyers better than he understood high

> **What is causing _you_ to feel stymied or diverted?**

end products and their buyers. The obvious solution was a shift towards selling the lines he understood. He had been extending credit unwisely, so he stopped doing that and went to a no-credit policy. These were the things that created frustration for him and changing them eliminated the frustration.

What is creating frustration for you right now? What is keeping you from attaining the success you want? What are your alternatives?

Step Two, develop and execute a positive plan of action. If I continue to do the same old things, I can expect the same old results. If I want different results, I have to change what I'm doing. Sounds awfully simple, doesn't it? Then why is it such a difficult concept for us to grasp? What are so many people

- *SWALLOW YOUR EGO*
- *ASK FOR HELP*
- *SEEK ADVICE*
- *SET GOALS*
- *GO INTO NEW AREAS*

making the same mistakes over and over and yet still expecting some new result?

It is the difference in having ten years of experience and having one year of experience ten times over. Repetitive action creates habits; exploring alternatives brings experience.

R.H. Macy changed his entire business philosophy. He agreed to stay in the retail business, but other than that, most of his business concepts changed. This required him to swallow his ego, ask for help, seek advice and set goals to go into what was for him uncharted waters.

> ***There is a direct correlation between cause and effect. We cannot change the effect, we can only alter the cause and watch how the effect changes.***

If you ever feel like pounding your fists on the table in frustration, take heart, you may be close to a breakthrough. This is also an indication that you are probably a 21.

Know Your Limitations

Know your limitations. Everyone has limitations. 21's know they cannot be the best at everything and part of their secret to success is to capitalize on their strengths and not fall victim to their limitations. 21's know their limitations and surround themselves with people who have complementary strengths to their weaknesses.

> *Lee Iacocca was the legendary CEO who turned around the Chrysler Corporation. His track record included a stint at the Ford Motor Company where he led the team that created the Mustang, one of the greatest automobile success stories in American history. At Chrysler, he used his understanding*

Chapter One: The Theory of 21

of automotive design to lead the company to create some new vehicles including the first minivan. But he also surrounded himself with a team of people who had strengths in his weak places. He brought in some phenomenal production engineers and financial wizards.

> **Do not surround yourself with "yes-men" or people who think like you...**

Iacocca knew his strengths and his weaknesses. He capitalized on his strengths and found people to shore up his weaknesses. Remember, too, that many of the people he brought in did not agree with all of his ideas. He wanted people who would challenge him, people who had different ideas. One of his most famous quotes remains, "IF I HAVE TWO EXECUTIVES WHO THINK ALIKE, I HAVE ONE TOO MANY EXECUTIVES."

Abe Plough wanted to sell. And, like most good salespeople, he wanted to make a lot of money. He decided the best way to accomplish this was to manufacture and sell his own product. He knew sales, he did not know much about developing or manufacturing products.

Plough paid a chemist $50 to mix fifty gallons of "Antiseptic Healing Oil", an elixir that was a "sure cure for any ill - man or beast". It was, of course, not quite as effective as advertised. Why would he use such an outrageous advertising slogan? Because the competitors were using similar slogans and the customers had come to expect such boasting.

Plough was a wise and prudent man. He realized that his strengths were in selling. What he needed was a high quality product - one that could be sold on its real assets.

After word of mouth ruined his business, Plough began selling popular products. The profits weren't as good but there were no more customers angrily demanding their money back either.

Abe Plough could not turn loose of the idea that combining manufacturing and selling was the key to making it big. Selling alone would provide a comfortable income but Plough wanted more. He had bigger dreams, just as you do, and he had limitations, as you do. He put together a plan and a few years later bought the St. Joseph Aspirin Company.

Later he would merge with a partner and form the Shering - Plough Corporation, which today has thirty different companies within its structure, each manufacturing products that the sales force can sell.

Plough became successful when he recognized his limitations and did something about them. More than just capitalizing on our strengths, we need to acknowledge our weaknesses and find ways to overcome them.

Once you know what you want and you are sure that having it is more important than **Take inventory** attaining it, then it is time for an inventory. What strengths do you have that will help you attain this goal? What weakness do you have that might prevent you from making it happen and what type of help will you need?

Once you know what you want and you are sure that having it is more important than attaining it, then it is time for an inventory. What strengths do you have that will help you attain this goal? What

Chapter One: The Theory of 21

weakness do you have that might prevent you from making it happen and what type of help will you need?

Once you know what talents, skills, contacts and other resources are needed, you can go about finding the people who will help you, the people I call the Twenty Ones. Their name is a reflection of their position in your quest for success. Here is my basic premise for persisting in your success; it's the Theory of 21:

> *FOR EVERY PERSON WHO WILL SAY YES, THERE ARE TWENTY WHO WILL SAY NO. FOR A POSITIVE RESPONSE YOU MUST FIND THE TWENTY-FIRST PERSON.*

Why is that whenever you or I have a good idea, a new idea, something that we know can be done and should be done, twenty out of twenty one people say, "You can't do that", "You shouldn't do that", or "You won't do that"? This is a natural reaction, believe it or not, based on several elements of human nature. As you will learn in this book, there are more people who are eager to stop you from succeeding than there are people willing to encourage your success. The encouragers are the 21's, the discouragers are the *20's*.

You will also learn how to recognize who the people are who will really help you, the 21's, and who the people are that will try to stop you, the *20's*. You will learn how to either neutralize or work around the *20's*, the human obstacles.

After the first edition of this book was published in 1983, people began writing to me and stopping me in airports to tell me their stories about the Theory of 21. Since then, I have observed more and more incidents of the Theory at work. When you have had some experience using the Theory of 21, you will be able to accomplish more of your objectives and accomplish them faster. Best of all, you will be able to teach others how they can succeed.

15

Choose to be a 21!

The Six Mistakes of Man according to Cicero

1. The delusion that personal gain is made by crushing others.

2. The tendency to worry about things that cannot be changed or corrected.

3. Insisting that a thing is impossible because we cannot accomplish it.

4. Refusing to set aside trivial preferences.

5. Neglecting development and refinement of the mind, and not acquiring the habit of reading and studying.

6. Attempting to compel others to believe and live as we do.

Cicero was a 21.

Chapter Two

The Quest for A Yes

*For every person who will say yes, there are **20** who will say no. For a positive response you must find the 21st person. - The Theory of 21*

The Theory of 21 applies in every aspect of your life. It applies at home. It applies in business, in marketing, in engineering, in manufacturing. The Theory also applies in education, to teachers and students. It applies in churches, civic groups, social organizations, and sororities and fraternities. In fact, the Theory applies to any universe of 21 people or more. The reason is: the Theory is a part of human nature.

I didn't invent the Theory of 21 - I merely recognized it for what it was. Like Sir Isaac Newton, who is said to have discovered gravity by observing the simple phenomenon of the falling of an apple, I don't necessarily like or dislike the Theory. I may not completely understand the "why" behind the Theory; I only attempt to explain the "what" of the Theory. The Theory has been in effect for a long time - at least since biblical days. There are records of 21 since the advent of written history. Just as gravity was in effect before we named it and began to study

> **The Theory of 21 is a part of human nature...**

17

it, the Theory of 21 has been in force, and now we can begin to study it, understand it, and use it.

We may not understand exactly why objects fall perpendicularly to the earth's surface - it certainly would be more interesting if they fell at forty-five-degree angles. We would probably all be better off if objects fell more slowly than they do. But God made gravity as it is, and that's that. All we can do is to use it to our advantage.

The same is true of the Theory of 21.

> **...use it to your advantage**

We need to learn to use it to our advantage at work, at home, and anytime there is something to be accomplished. That's what this book is all about. After reading this book and observing people in a manner that may be unfamiliar to you now, you will learn to discern which people can really help you and which will actually try to stop or delay you. Then you will be using the Theory of 21 to be more successful at almost anything you attempt.

Now, gravity started out as a theory and, after a convincing sales campaign, became the LAW of gravity. I am enough of a 21 to believe that the Theory of 21 should receive the same notoriety. So, the first edition of this material was published as The Theory of 21 and now it has become a Law!

Acceptance of the Law of gravity caused dramatic changes to take place. Babies experimenting with gravity gave rise to unbreakable baby bottles. Young children testing the effects of gravity caused the creation of the training wheel industry. Teenagers challenging the effects of gravity as a form of recreation have caused a surge in the sales of skateboards, elbow pads, knee pads, Ace bandages, and casts.

Chapter Two: A Quest for A Yes

> As the Theory of 21 becomes accepted, we can expect dramatic changes in our lives and in the world.

The Theory is based on my observations of a seemingly illogical behavior pattern, one demonstrated over and over by a majority of people. I have seen this behavior in all races, both sexes, all strata of management, and every social and economic class. The goal of these people is to accomplish nothing and to make sure that everyone around them accomplishes nothing. Their behavior is *intended* to accomplish nothing. It may require a great deal of time and effort, but their goal is to ensure that nothing gets done. Does it amaze you that people would spend enormous amounts of time and energy to keep things from happening? After all, couldn't the same resources be used to make great things happen?

> **YOU THINK LIKE A WINNER AND SOMETIMES YOU WONDER WHY EVERYONE DOES NOT THINK THAT WAY**

You think like a winner. You think energy should be spent in making good things happen. Have you ever wondered why others don't think that way? The answer is in the Theory of 21.

You will see, in this book and all around you, evidence of this Theory in action. You will observe enormous amounts of resources being expended, in seemingly worthwhile causes that result in nothing. And these people consider themselves to be successes because the goal set was the goal achieved - nothing.

You may be asking yourself, "Why is this happening?" When you have finished this book, you will understand why.

The pattern is always the same (although it may be masked, as we will discuss later). For every undertaking there will be *20* people who will find some reason why it cannot be done. They will identify something that is merely an obstacle, declare it to be immovable, stand by it, and defend it rigidly. The obstacle soon becomes the dead end. I call these people "*20's*."

20's have the ability to take even the smallest or flimsiest obstacle and turn it into an absolute dead end. There is little that anyone can do to move *20's* away from his or her obstacles. Sometimes this ability results from Twentyism, which is a belief - almost a religion - that these people follow zealously. Other times it shows up in the form of Twentyitis, which is an infectious disease that permeates the population. It is easily contracted by the less ambitious and is difficult to cure. Those afflicted with Twentyitis, Twentyism, or apathy can spread it. In all cases, it flourishes on obstacles.

Obstacles come in three flavors: can't be, shouldn't be, and won't be. Some of the more frequent *"can't be's"* are:

It can't be done because . . .
- we've never done it that way before.
- it won't work, don't ask me why.
- it costs too much.
- it violates Rule 97360A7, Section IV A.1.
- it just can't.

Some popular *"shouldn't be's"* are:

It shouldn't be done because . . .
- it would set a precedent.
- everybody would want one.
- it wouldn't be in the best interests of the customer.
- it just shouldn't.

Chapter Two: A Quest for A Yes

And finally:

> ***It won't be done because...***
> - so-and-so won't approve it.
> - such-and-such department won't allow it.
> - nobody will push it.
> - it just won't.

Until now, very few people have tried to find or be the 21st person. But that is changing. A growing number of people in all walks of life are accepting the challenge to accomplish the difficult in order to achieve the impossible. Many of these people were stimulated by the successes of other 21's. Others were motivated by the desire to survive, to overcome the threats of competition, economic perils, and other dangers. Whatever the stimulation, 21's have one thing in common: they *achieve*.

America was founded by groups of 21's. Beginning with Columbus, whose ***20's*** included heads of state and noted scientists, this underdeveloped country came to be a world power because enough people understood and withstood the Theory of 21.

Once you understand the impact of being a 21, you'll grasp the *importance* of being a 21. Become a 21 and YOU WILL MAKE A DIFFERENCE! Regardless of your definition of success, despite what anyone else may have told you about your ability to achieve great things, you will make a difference in your own life and in the lives of others.

That's also what this book is about: becoming a 21 and making an impact on your family, your church, your business, your country, and even the world.

Sound like a lot of hype? When you finish this book you will not only be able to recognize the *20's* and the 21's in virtually every situation, but you will also be able to see the impact that the 21's are having. And best of all, you will learn how you, with your current capabilities, can be a 21.

Why should you believe that?

Let's look at some examples, starting with good old Christopher Columbus. You remember the story from grammar school: everybody except Columbus and a few other misfits believed that the world was flat and that if you sailed far enough toward the west you'd fall off. (Remember, it was Columbus and a few others; we'll come back to that later.) Columbus believed that if he sailed far enough toward the west he'd wind up east of where he started. That was pretty radical thinking for his time.

To prove his Theory, Columbus needed ships and money. He had neither, and no apparent means to get them. So Columbus set out to find another 21 who would help him. He was trying to accomplish the difficult (find a 21 who will help) in order to achieve the impossible (prove that the world isn't flat). Among the *20's* he encountered were astronomers who could prove him wrong scientifically. Experienced seamen could prove him wrong from their knowledge of the sea, and all sorts of political leaders could find no merit in such a foolish undertaking. And, of course, there were economists who demonstrated the fiscal irresponsibility of it all.

Was Christopher Columbus right?

There were many others who questioned the mental stability of Mr. Columbus, as well as the validity of his assumption. Columbus had some formidable *20's* opposing his project. But he was a 21 who needed another 21, and he continued his pursuit.

Chapter Two: A Quest for A Yes

Columbus's quest led him to Queen Isabella, a 21. She, too, had to overcome her own set of *20's* - the fifteenth-century equivalents of presidential advisers. Each of these advisers had solid reasons why the project should not be started. But the Queen persevered, as Columbus had, and the project was sold, and completed, and everybody lived happily ever after, right?

Not exactly, because, interestingly, Columbus was not completely right. He had sold the project based on the idea that by sailing west he would end up east - in India. From India he could bring many much sought after luxuries to be marketed at a tremendous profit. What Columbus didn't realize was that there was a three-thousand-mile continent in the way. Once he reached land, he compounded his mistake by referring to the native population as "Indians" and by attempting to trade beads for things the "Indians" had never seen, much less produced.

These minor mistakes, in the control of a 21, were not enough to spoil the whole project. Imagine what a *20* would have done. A *20* would probably never have attempted the voyage in the first place. But assuming he had, the *20* would have returned and admitted that he was wrong - you couldn't get to India by sailing west. The entire project would have been abandoned, and America would not have been discovered for another few hundred years, when some cruise line made it a stop on one of their itineraries.

It all turned out all right, of course. This nation was developed and eventually gave the world Big Macs and the banjo. The important thing to remember is that Columbus had an idea, he was a 21, and he sought and found another 21 to make his idea happen.

You can do the same!

Now, what about the others who also believed, as Columbus did, that the world was round? We do not have their names recorded in history because they never accomplished anything of historical significance. They also had good, valid ideas, but when all was said and done, a lot was said and nothing was done. The world rewards accomplishment.

Here's a question, were these others *20's* or 21's? I believe that they were initially 21's but somewhere on their trek past the *20's*, they accepted the "can't," "shouldn't" or "won't" and allowed the obstacle to become the dead end. This illustrates an important aspect of the Theory of *20* One: 21's don't always win. A *21 can* always win, but the purpose of *20's* is to prevent the success of the 21's, and, occasionally, they win one.

For years after Columbus's exploits, those who had given in to the *20's* regularly slapped their foreheads with the palms of their hands. And they began many conversations with "If only . . ." Do you know people who are regularly saying, "If only..."? These are some of the *20's* in your life.

> **The lament of the 20:**
> ***"If only..."***

What about the *20's*? Did they lament their misjudgment? Did they witness the accomplishment of a 21 and vow to become 21's themselves? Not on your life! You'll see why later.

> ***Being a 20 or a 21 is a choice... You can be either***

There is an interesting difference in the way that *20's* and 21's celebrate their victories. Since the goal of the *20* is to prevent something from happening, they celebrate by heaving a great sigh of relief. 21's, on the other hand, celebrate by celebrating! They smile a lot and relish the glory of the moment.

Chapter Two: A Quest for A Yes

Remember that the goal of the *20* is to accomplish NOTHING, and success for him brings just that - NOTHING.

Now, what about you? Are you among the *20's* or the 21's? Which do you want to be? Understand that YOU CAN BE EITHER! It's a matter of choice.

Do you believe that today, in the twentieth century, it is possible that you could discover a new land or disprove accepted scientific principles? This is an important question, so answer it in your mind before reading any further.

If your answer included the remark "There are no more lands to discover," then you're thinking like a *20*. And what's even more tragic, you're using the exact same words that your predecessors used five hundred years ago. Stop thinking like that!

Maybe you're not interested in becoming an explorer or revolutionizing science. I know I'm not, at least not right now. But there are things you want to accomplish. Once you pass the *20's* and shake off the mind-set of the *20's*, you will realize your goal. Believe it!

THOUGHTS ALWAYS PRECEDE ACTIONS

This is more than just positive thinking - it is also positive planning and positive action. Thinking is essential as a prerequisite to action, but thinking alone accomplishes little. I'm an avid believer in positive thinking and a fan of the modern father of that philosophy, Norman Vincent Peale. Thought always precedes action. Positive thoughts result in positive action. Negative thoughts never result in positive action. Therefore, positive thinking is essential, but positive thinking does not produce positive results. It takes positive action to produce results.

The formula for successful accomplishments sounds incredibly simple:

> **POSITIVE THINKING + POSITIVE ACTION = POSITIVE RESULTS**

How could anyone miss that? Yet, it happens all day, every day. Amazing, huh?

All of the positive thinking in the world that is not accompanied by positive action will yield little or, most likely, nothing. Shortly after the first version of this book came out, a young man came and said he wanted to be my protégé. He was really into affirmations, positive thinking, meditation, visualization and imaging. He was not into hard work. He thought, talked and meditated himself into a thousand schemes for success. At the time, we were both down to our last few dollars trying to make a success in the speaking profession. A few months later I drove over to his apartment in my new Jaguar to help him load his belongings out of the street where his landlord had thrown them. His unwillingness to put action behind his thoughts had led him to a situation that cannot be described as successful.

> **If hard work were the key to success, everyone would want to be a ditch digger**

If hard work were the key to success, everyone would want to be a dishwasher in a barbecue restaurant. Still, effort is rewarded in kind: the more we do, the more positive things happen.

This assumes, of course, that the thoughts that accompany the effort are positive ones.

A salesperson goes to his manager and says, "All right. I will make a sales call on Acme Widgets. They're not going to buy from us. They never have and they never will. But if you tell me I have to make the

Chapter Two: A Quest for A Yes

call, I'll make the call. Just don't expect much." How do you think that call is going to go? You can write the call report right now, can't you? It will say, "Told you so."

> "SELF-IMPOSED LIMITATIONS" IS A REDUNDANT TERM:
> ALL LIMITATIONS ARE SELF IMPOSED. LEARN TO STRETCH BEYOND YOUR PERCEIVED LIMITATIONS.

The child who has been encouraged by his or her parent to do something significant, cannot be allowed to respond with something like, "I can't do that". If it is allowed, the results are already determined. Part of building a 21 is not only supporting their ideas but also stimulating their ideas and encouraging them to stretch beyond their perceived limitations.

How many times have we come close to using such a negative approach to something we are about to undertake? We make the phone call "knowing" the person will not be receptive to our ideas. We meet the person and can "tell" by their response that they will not be interested in doing what we want them to do.

Positive thinking does not create some *ethereal positive karma in the celestial realm*, as some teach. It creates an attitude in the way we talk, our choice of words, our body language and a host of other subliminal things that will influence the outcome. Our positive thinking has as much impact on others as it does on us.

> *POSITIVE THOUGHT IS THE IGNITION, THE BEGINNING.*
> *POSITIVE ACTION IS THE PROCESS.*

Thinking creates ideas, and ideas are cheap! Sit down by yourself for a few minutes and allow your mind to run in

Sometimes the ideas of the 20 are actually better than the ideas of the 21 – they are just less likely to happen

neutral. You may be surprised at how many ideas come into your thoughts. Then try sitting down with a group and brainstorming for the same amount of time. The result will be that even more ideas will come to you. But until something is done with those ideas, they are useless and worthless.

Do *20's* ever have ideas? Yes, and quite often their idea is the same as the idea of a 21. Sometimes their ideas are even better. However, the *20* will think about the idea in terms of why it couldn't, shouldn't or won't be done and will not take any action until a 21 tries to make a reality out of the idea. The 21 looks at the same idea as an opportunity and evaluates the possibilities of the idea, and then determines how he will pursue it and make it happen.

You will need an action plan. If you've never developed an action plan or if your imagination needs a little jogging, here's an idea to start you off. Take two sheets of paper. Number one sheet from 1 to *20* and set it aside. This is the sheet on which you will list your *20's* who said no, and why they said it.

At the top of the other sheet write the following sentences and fill in the blanks, as shown on the sample on the following page.

Chapter Two: A Quest for A Yes

"I will accomplish the seemingly impossible goal of

_____
_____ by: _____ (DATE) _____ .

To accomplish that goal by that date, I will need to accomplish the following tactics:

1.
2.
3.
4.
5.
6.
7.
8.
9.
10.

The other list is your list of **"*20's* Who Said No"** and *why* they said no. We need to track the reasons why people are saying something cannot be done because there may be a valid reason for us to modify our goal.

For instance, if a young person set a goal to become president of the United States by the time they reached the age of twenty five, many people would let them know that the Constitution forbids that from happening. This does not mean that the person cannot be President, only that to achieve the goal in the stated time frame will require a Constitutional amendment - a difficult but not impossible task.

Here's what a typical **"20's Who Said No"** sheet looks like:

20's WHO SAID NO	THEIR REASON
1	
2	
3	
4	
5	
6	
7	
8	
9	
10	
11	
12	
13	
14	
15	
16	
17	
18	
19	
20	

If the same reason for not achieving occurs frequently on your list, take a close look at it. There may be some validity in the objection. For instance, if many of the people you have approached with your idea have given the same objection, there may be some validity to the objection. This is not a reason to stop seeking the goal; it is an indication that a creative alternative may be needed.

Chapter Two: A Quest for A Yes

As you read this book, you will be able to list some of the steps you will need to take to accomplish the tactics that will lead to achieving the seemingly impossible goal. As you encounter the ***20's***, the people who will try to prevent you from achieving your objective, you will probably identify additional steps that need to be taken.

As an example: suppose you wanted to achieve the impossible goal of having a book published. The tasks that must be accomplished to do that would include writing the book, finding a publisher that handles that type of book, and convincing an editor to review the manuscript. The steps involved might include buying a few hundred sheets of paper, conducting some interviews, and talking to some people in the publishing business. As you approach some of these people, you will learn rather quickly that some of them are ***20's*** and are determined to stop your book. Don't take it personally. They have probably turned down better works than yours. But don't let their obstacle become your dead end. Just note on your sheet of paper that another step will be required, and move ahead. Be sure to put that person's name on the list of ***20's*** so that you can keep track of how many rejections you've received. Remember, you must have **20** rejections before you find the 21.

The 21 Worksheet that I prepared for the project of writing the original version of this book looked something like this:

I will achieve the impossible goal of <u>having my book published within six months.</u>

In order to do that, I must first accomplish the difficult tasks of <u>finishing the manuscript, identifying a publisher, and having my manuscript reviewed by the right editor.</u>

The steps I will take are:

1. Determine to be a 21 throughout this project.
2. Complete the manuscript by (date).
3. Identify and contact 21 publishers by (date).
4. Adjust my presentation and my plan according to the input I receive from the contacts I make.
5.
6.
7.
8.
9.
10.

You'll notice several things about my plan that may be of interest to you. First of all, I assigned deadlines for the most important items on the list. Also, I determined to contact 21 publishers when I only need one. The reason for that is my strong conviction of the validity of the Theory of 21. As good as this book is, *20* of the first 21 people I talk to about it will give me a reason why it will not make it into print. If by some chance more than one publisher likes the book, then I'll be in a better position to negotiate.

Also, note from my list that there is plenty of room for adjustment. In the beginning, there were many unidentified steps. My plan was that as I moved through the *20's*, I would see the things that must be done that I could not see in the beginning. A *20* stops at the first sign of opposition: a 21 learns from opposition, gets past it, and moves on.

So, what happened?

Many people and the reference books I consulted indicated that the process would take weeks, months or maybe a year. After several weeks I could expect the first rejection letters to arrive in my

Chapter Two: A Quest for A Yes

mailbox. Within a few months, according to the experts, I could expect some kind of offer if indeed the book had any potential.

On a Wednesday I took twenty-one proposals to the post office, said a prayer and went home to wait. On Friday I received a phone call from an editor in a New York publishing company. She wanted to know if the book was still available. I said it was. She asked me not to do anything with it until Monday because her publisher would read my proposal over the weekend.

Now what could I do? No one else had called!

On Monday I had a contract. How long did it take me to sell the book using the Theory of 21? Six days. What do you think started coming in the mail after that? Rejection letters - twenty of them! Some were obviously form letters, some had checked the box that best described their reason for rejecting, and others were positive responses from publishers who thought the book had merit but who had filled their list for the season.

One publisher sent a post card rejection. The mailman knew I had been rejected! Did any of that matter? No, because the last rejection letter came after the book was named Book of the Month at the local B. Dalton's Book Store.

It is important to write down your plans on paper. I don't really understand why, but writing it down solidifies the plan in your subconscious mind and really helps to make things happen. Having a written guide is also very beneficial in keeping you on track. The first entry on my list of tasks is always to determine to be a 21 throughout the project. I am always surprised when someone who I was sure was a 21 turns out to be a *20*. When this happens, I occasionally have to go back to my list to remind myself that I am a

Put your plans on paper

33

21 and that no *20*, no matter how much I may respect the person, is going to make a *20* out of me.

Review your lists occasionally. Seeing the progress you are making will encourage you to do more, and the lists will provide direction to channel your renewed energy. This is especially important when you are discouraged; reviewing the list will remind you that you are making progress. When you review your list of the *20's*, try to see if there is a pattern to the type of people listed there. This may give you a clue as to where to look for your 21.

Also, keeping the list of **"20's Who Said No"** will provide an accurate account of the number of contacts you've made. About the time you're contacting the tenth or twelfth person, it will seem as though you must have gone through at least *20* people. The list will confirm that you are close but not quite there.

Understand why people are saying no

There is a difference between strategy and tactics. If you have a background in the military, you may recall that a strategy mighty be to take an enemy position. The tactics that would be necessary to affect the strategy might include bombing a supply line, performing reconnaissance in the surrounding area, and capturing smaller positions that would be of "strategic" importance. In the corporate world, particularly in marketing, we establish objectives (strategies) and then define a marketing plan (tactics) to achieve those objectives.

At home, we decide what we want to accomplish and then we break down the activities that will be required to make the success happen. For instance, suppose you want to improve your living environment. One strategy would be to paint and paper the rooms. Another would be to refurnish the rooms. Still another might be to have a great home entertainment center. The tactics for making this happen would include looking at magazines, reading stereo magazines, etc.

Chapter Two: A Quest for A Yes

It is important to define the exact goal of your project. If you don't know what you're shooting for, how will you know when you hit it?

Then it is equally important to clearly establish the strategy for achieving the goal. If you don't know where you're going, it doesn't matter how you get there.

After you have your sights set on a target, then develop a plan and follow it. You know where you're going, you know how to get there, and now, with a plan, you translate all the "idea-ism" into action. This is where ideas begin to become reality.

In the Theory of 21 there is the goal, there are the difficult tasks, which equate to strategies, and there are the steps, which are the same as tactics. This process is outlined, for each project, by the 21's. The *20's* fly by the seat of their pants - no plans, no strategies, no tactics and, of course, no goals. *20's* stay in the react mode, while 21's are the ones who act. Find someone who knows where he or she is going and how they plan to get there, and you're probably talking to a 21.

READY – FIRE – AIM

21's are also known for making things happen quickly. The term "Ready - Fire - Aim" was first used to describe 21's. They launch their ideas, they monitor the progress and they make adjustments as necessary. By the time the goal is realized, the 21's are usually off on another quest. Others have trouble keeping up with the 21's because they move so quickly.

Henry Kaiser was a ship builder. When World War Two broke out, the United States needed more ships than the current shipyards could build. Kaiser pioneered a fast start manufacturing process that allowed the ships to be built as the shipyards were built. New vessels were launched in record time from docks where the ship building facilities did not even exist previously.

On one occasion, Eleanor Roosevelt was asked to christen a new ship. As she drew back the champagne bottle, the ship slid into the water. It all happened so quickly that Mrs. Roosevelt could not hit any part of the ship.

THINGS HAPPEN QUICKLY WHEN 21'S ARE IN CHARGE; SOMETIMES A LITTLE TOO QUICKLY.

The automobile line included models that had an aluminum four-cylinder engine, front wheel drive, fiberglass and aluminum body panels, torsion bar suspension and the best gas mileage of any production automobile. They sold miserably because they were ahead of their time. It was the line of cars from the Kaiser-Frazier Corporation.

Joe Frazer and Henry Kaiser were both successful industrialists. Frazer was a successful supplier to the automobile industry; Kaiser was in the steel business. Both were 21's. However, when Kaiser announced his plans to build a post war automobile for the common man, Frazer was widely quoted in the papers with his perception that the idea was absurd and impractical.

The two men finally met face to face and, as often happens when 21's meet, within a matter of days the Kaiser-Frazer Corporation was formed. The synergy between the two men brought balance to the organization and at the same time accelerated the production processes.

Chapter Two: A Quest for A Yes

Just because there are no 21's in a given industry or there seems to be no need for them on specific projects, don't be lulled into thinking that there really is

> **Don't be afraid to be the first 21 – someone has to do it, it might as well be you!**

no need for them. Some pretty startling things have been accomplished in some seemingly unimpressive places, once a 21 steps in. Usually the first 21 to tackle an area dominated by *20's* comes away with the lion's share of the benefits. So don't be afraid to be the first 21 on your block.

Companies and even entire industries can become complacent. The attitude of mature organizations can often be described as "been there, done that". When new ideas are presented, the response is that we've already done that or something similar. If something similar has not been attempted in the past, there must be a reason. Either way, the new idea needs to be shelved.

> *The hamburger industry was already alive and well before McDonald's was born. But because Ray Kroc thought he had a better way to market burgers, tens of billions of hamburgers have passed under the "Golden Arches" and another 21 laughed all the way to the bank.*

> *Three long-established networks controlled the television industry until a country boy from Atlanta launched his cable network. Very few experts gave this venture any kind of a chance. After all, its beginnings were a local, fading UHF station, and even good UHF stations were no threat to the giants. But Ted Turner is a 21, uses 21's and does not accept negative thinking. His philosophy also exemplifies the thinking of most 21's:*

> **LEAD, FOLLOW, OR GET OUT OF THE WAY.**

*A couple of young men began building personal computers in their garage before the experts thought the market was ready for them. They were entering a market dominated domestically by the giant IBM Corporation and saturated by foreign products from apparently superior, high technology Japanese companies. Yet their product, "**Apple**", almost became as synonymous with personal computers as "Frigidaire" did with refrigerators. Like most people, I assumed that IBM or Honeywell would make the most important innovations in computers. You just never know where or when another 21 will show up.*

Nothing can stop a 21, not even another 21. I always enjoy watching two or more 21's going after the same goal. In times like that, the absolute best in human nature emerges. We see the best competing with the best, and what emerges is performance that exceeds anyone's expectations. When 21's compete with other 21's, they surprise even themselves.

> **Nothing can stop a 21 – not even another 21**

Two brothers, both 21's, ran the family business. One day, after months of disagreements over several business issues, the brothers decided to go their separate ways. They sold the family business, a shoe manufacturing company, and split the profits evenly. Since the footwear they had been producing enjoyed an enviable reputation for quality and popularity, the profits were substantial. Each of the brothers could have retired. But that is not the way of the 21's.

Since what they each understood was manufacturing shoes, they opened new shoe companies. Adolf Dassler called his shoes "Adidas" and his brother, Rudolf, called his "Pumas".

Who you define as a competitor says a lot about who you think you are. Are you going up against those who would challenge you to

Chapter Two: A Quest for A Yes

achieve greater accomplishments, or are you competing only against those that you can beat with your current skills?

Once, when I was searching for a job, I was offered a position with a company marketing a product that, I was told, "had no competition." That statement was the main reason I declined the offer. How can you motivate people to sell, really sell, if there is no competition? And how do you ever "win" a sale? Where's the challenge?

Most 21's would rather compete with other 21's than with *20's*. Most tennis players and golfers would rather compete with strong contenders than with someone they can easily defeat. There is no fun in easy wins. There is also no growth and little challenge in the simple victories.

RIGHT NOW, SET YOUR GOAL.

Write your goal down on a piece of paper, as we discussed earlier. Don't wait for a chance to have it typed, and don't worry about the stationery. Find something to write on and with, and put your goal on paper. The back of an envelope or a napkin will do great. Seeing your goal in writing will do something to you and for you.

Decide what the first strategy must be, and write it down.

Now list the action steps (tactics) that you will undertake to make this difficult task happen.

As you read this book, you will learn how to recognize 21's, Negative *20's*, and Positive *20's*. You will begin to see who you already know that is going to help you and who isn't. As you identify the 21's, you may find it necessary to change your tactical plan. That's okay.

Even before you have finished reading this entire book, you may embark on your quest. That's good: the sooner you get started, the better. When you finish the book (and be sure that you do), make sure that you are in motion, seeking your goal.

> **Ideas are cheap – and useless**

Very little happens by itself, you must make it happen. Remember, ideas alone are useless. If you want to build a better mousetrap, start designing a prototype. If you want to become a concert violinist, get the fiddle out and start practicing. If you want to write a symphony, turn off the television, take out some score sheets, and sit down at the piano.

STUDY – LEARN - DEMONSTRATE

Want to become the vice-president of marketing? Start doing the things that vice-presidents of marketing do. My formula for success in any corporate situation is: STUDY--LEARN--DEMONSTRATE. *Study* what a VP of Marketing is and does. *Learn* what you must know to qualify for the position, and then *learn* what you must know to qualify for the position. Finally, *demonstrate* that you understand the position by performing like a VP of Marketing. If the position you desire is three promotions away, then map out a strategy for each promotion. Start performing like the next higher position's best performer. Ask yourself what a high performer in the next rank ahead of you is doing to distinguish himself or herself, and do that. If you cannot do what the star is doing, find out why and correct it.

If your desire is to be the top salesperson in the company, make that your goal. The first strategy for you is to increase your sales. How are you going to do that? What is your plan? If the top salesperson is making an average of five calls a day, make six. If the top salesperson is closing 50 percent of his or her calls, close 60 percent. If you don't

> **No one should want your success more than you do**

Chapter Two: A Quest for A Yes

believe you can find a way to close a higher percentage, you're a **20**. Pass this book on to someone who can use it. But before you do, check the final chapter.

No one has as strong a desire for you to succeed as you do. Success requires action. How soon can you start?

I once did one of my "guitar talks," where I sing, play, and motivate all in one sitting, for a group in Atlanta. Afterward a man came up to me and said, "I wish I could play a guitar like that." I looked at him and said, "Maybe I can help you. Tell me what happened the last time you tried." He smiled sheepishly and admitted that he'd never tried. Did he really wish he could play the guitar?

Surprisingly, he did. I heard him playing in public less than a year later, and he was pretty good. So watch out, Chet Atkins, there's a 21 loose in your backyard.

You've heard it before:

WHETHER YOU THINK YOU CAN OR
WHETHER YOU THINK YOU CAN'T,
EITHER WAY YOU'RE RIGHT.

The difference between the *20's* and the 21's is that the 21's think they can, and they act on that belief. As a 21 you can expect challenges and conquests, vipers and victories, war and wins.

A 21 EXPECTS THE BEST AND ACHIEVES IT

A 20 EXPECTS NOTHING AND ACHIEVES IT.

Make your decision and get started.

41

Chapter Three

The Negative Twenty (-20)

What happens when you have a new idea? After thinking it through and working out any weaknesses that might cause it to fail, you begin seeking the opinions of others. You want to "bounce some ideas off" a friend so you take them to lunch. In your golfing or shopping time with people you trust, you talk about your idea and you look for their support and suggestions.

Too many people, and in fact most people, will use this opportunity to tell you why your idea cannot, should not and will not happen. In

> **There are an amazing number of people with an incredible ability to find reasons why things cannot be done**

the next chapter you will see that some of them will even sound supportive as they try to kill your idea. In this chapter we will deal with those people who tell you right up front that your idea is without merit. These are the same people who will offer you valid sounding reasons (not valid reasons, only valid *sounding* reasons) why your idea cannot be accomplished.

There are an amazing number of people with an incredible ability to find reasons why things cannot be done. No matter how determined a person might be, these people will spend enormous amounts of time and energy trying to convince others that any new idea cannot, should not and will not be done. I call these folks the Negative Twenties, *(-20's)*.

They have one goal in life: accomplishing nothing. They do not intend to accomplish anything new and they will do everything in their power to see to that no one else accomplishes anything either. When nothing happens, it is a tribute to the *-20's*.

You know these people, don't you?

> *Thomas Watson had an idea. His idea was to use the state of the art electronics of the day to build a mathematical processor using the binary code system. This device would be able to process large numbers - larger than had been processed before, and at speeds never before accomplished. As a result, this machine would calculate and test formulas and assumptions to greater and greater depths.*

Watson's device, which he called a computer, would make difficult tasks easy and impossible tasks possible. As he began sharing his idea, he met his share of *-20's*. As we analyze the *-20's* Tom Watson encountered, we will see some of the tactics and strategies they use, the same ones they will use on you. We will also see how the *-20's* claim they were right and Watson was wrong. Here are the steps the *-20's* tend to follow in thwarting the efforts of *21's* like you.

Step One: Kill the Concept

First of all, the *-20's* shoot down the entire idea. For Thomas Watson's *-20's*, this was easy. There had never been a computer like this before. Humans have an innate fear of the unknown. All the *-20's* had to do was to point out that this had never been done before,

Chapter Three: The Negative Twenty (-20)

"and there must be a reason for that". As absurd as that sounds, many people are still using that argument today to stop the *21's*.

"If your idea is such a good one, why hasn't anyone thought of it before? Won't you look silly when you find out that someone else has done it or there is a valid reason why it won't work?" Do you see how this approach plays on the typical fears people have? Most of us do not want to be wrong and when we are occasionally wrong we would rather no one knew about it.

This step is where most would-be *21's* stop. They buy into the invalid argument of the *-20's* and stop pursuing their dream. The *-20* claims success because, once again, nothing happens.

> *You probably know that the McCormick Reaper revolutionized agriculture in the United States and later in the rest of the world. What you may not know is that the product and the company were miserable failures at first even though the country was an agriculturally based economy at the time. In fact, Cyrus McCormick went bankrupt.*
>
> *The people who had financed his venture were 21's who became -20's who were eventually convinced that he would never succeed. They took his farm and all of his possessions, except for one. They declared his reaper to be worthless and let him keep it.*

The "worthless" McCormick reaper revolutionized agriculture and played a major role in making the United States a world leader in food production.

Step Two: Kill the Process

45

Once his *-20's* realized that Thomas Watson would continue his pursuit of the computer, they moved to step two. They would attempt to explain the difficulty and complexity of creating the device Watson imagined. If killing the concept does not work, the *-20* will try to show that the path to attaining the goal is too difficult to make the goal worthwhile.

Throughout history, the *–20's* have been successful at stopping *21's* by using the discouraging method of detailing how difficult the implementation process would be. The true *21's* are the ones who persisted despite the formidable task that their vision presented.

Remember, at one point in history, someone sat down and said, "Look, here is what we are going to do. We are going to have running water in every house in town. This will require us to build a huge reservoir, massive pumping stations and then bury pipes along every street in the city! Won't this be great?"

Many of the products and services that we take for granted today were once considered to be crazy and impossible

Or what about the person who proposed making electricity available to everyone? "Okay, here is what we will do. First, we build a dam and a hydroelectric plant. Then we cut down a zillion pine trees, strip off the bark and branches and soak them in creosote for a few days. Then, every hundred feet or so, all over town, we will dig holes twelve fee deep and set the poles. Then, we will have a few hundred workers go out with a few thousand miles of wire and connect all of the poles. Then, we will tell all of the citizens to buy wire and fixtures and wire their entire house. Then, we will connect them up and all we have to do after that is hire an army of people to go around each month, read the meters, send out bills and collect the money. Simple!"

Chapter Three: The Negative Twenty (-20)

Today we take electricity, running water, natural gas, telephone, cable television and host of other universal services for granted. We rarely give a thought to what the *21* who started the process must have gone through.

Again for Watson's *-20's*, using this step was easy. Watson's device would require tens of thousands of vacuum tubes. Each vacuum tube would require power and would generate heat that would require even more power to dissipate. The tubes would depend on each other and the failure of one would cause others to become inoperative. Because of their delicacy and complexity, the tubes would be expensive to buy and to maintain. And, of course, all of this would require manpower - highly paid electronics manpower.

The complexity of the process was exaggerated by the complexity of the components of the system. This should have been an easy win for Mr. Watson's *-20's*, but Watson persisted. His *-20's* then went to step three.

Step Three: Admit The Idea Is Good - For Someone Else

The *-20* typically becomes desperate at this point. They will actually begin sounding something like a *21*! Can you imagine? They begin acknowledging that the idea may, in fact, have validity. In fact, someone else will make it happen.

> **When a –20 makes a positive statement, you can be sure there is an "if" in there somewhere**

Watson's *-20's* had a cake walk here. There were already some major electronics manufacturers who would be the ideal organizations to make this "computer thing" happen, if it was going to happen at all. Surely Westinghouse and General Electric were working on their versions. And what about the vacuum tube manufacturers? If a single computer would bring sales of tens of thousands of tubes, wouldn't it be in the best interest of the tube makers to develop this machine?

Do you notice a common thread in these statements? It's the word "if". *-20's* predicate positive statements with "if". *21's* do not. The support of the idea is diluted by the inference that the idea has at least a limited chance of success.

Westinghouse and General Electric had two of the finest research and development operations in the world. Both focused on consumer products and the personal computer has become one of the best selling and most profitable consumer product lines in history. Surely these giants could see the value of the computer, *if* there was one.

When was the last time you saw a Westinghouse computer or a GE laser printer?

The folks at Westinghouse and GE were doing what they do best: they were expanding their product lines to address the needs of their target markets. A *21* knows this. However, a budding *21* might not know this and, consequently, might believe the *-20* who is telling them that only the big boys can accomplish the goals the *21* has in mind.

Later, Steven Jobs and Steve Wozniac would try to create the Apple Computer Company using a user-friendlier interface to create a larger demand for the computers, maybe even personal computers. They were told that Thomas Watson's company, IBM, would create a personal computer, *if* there were a market for one. In fact, IBM was still building and trying to sell their larger machines while the sophistication and capabilities of the PC's were making the big iron obsolete. Eventually, the IBM machines would have

-20's can come up with hundreds of valid-sounding reasons why you will not succeed

Chapter Three: The Negative Twenty (-20)

remarkably similar user interfaces as the Apple.

-20's can come up with hundreds of valid sounding ideas. You're either too old or too young, too early or too late, too smart or not smart enough. The *-20's* use whatever will work. None of these are valid reasons.

> *She was 38 years old. She had long since given up on her dream of becoming an entertainer. The only work she could find with her limited education and skills was scrubbing floors in New York. A chance passing of a mirror gave her the opportunity to see how despondent she looked and how tattered her clothes had become. She vowed to improve her life. Too old to be taken seriously in the field of entertainment she wanted, she tried another - comedy. You know her as Phyllis Diller.*

> *He had a third grade education. He had never held a steady job, only odd jobs. His dream of having his own restaurant was finally reached when he was well into his fifties. What he did not know was that a major highway was being built that would cause the travelers who frequented his restaurant to bypass him all together. At the age of 60 he was broke; his business had failed. But Harlan Sanders tried again. His recipe for Kentucky Fried Chicken, or KFC, and the booming interest in franchising made Colonel Sanders a wealthy and successful man.*

Your idea is for you - it is not for someone else. Unless you choose to give it away, it remains yours for the taking. It does not matter what others are telling you. If they say you're too young or too old, forget it. What if they say, "The big guys will do it"? Ignore it – the idea is yours.

Your idea is for you

Wilson Harrell was one of my favorite 21's. He never met a challenge he didn't like or a "no" he couldn't change. He bought a company that had a product known as Formula 409, a general purpose cleaner. Wilson saw potential.

He bought the company and began to market the remarkable cleaner nationwide. As a result, Formula 409 captured 5% of the cleaning products market and a whopping 50% of the spray cleaner market.

The good news was that 409 was making a lot of money, both in revenues and in profits. The bad news was that it woke a sleeping giant, Proctor and Gamble.

Seeing the success of 409, P&G decided to launch their own product called Cinch. Harrell was concerned since P&G could afford to spend more on advertising, market research and promotion than 409 made in total revenue. They could easily force him out of business; at the very least his market share would take a significant hit.

It was David against Goliath, but just like in the Bible, this David knew Goliath's weakness.

P&G's market research indicated strong potential for Cinch. They would test their findings in the Denver market. Knowing that the giant of giants was entering your market, how would you react? What if the –20's were gleefully pointing out that the big boys were coming?

Harrell understood his foe and went into action. He immediately stopped promoting his product in the Denver market. That's right, he stopped pushing it. He even quietly encouraged retailers to stop restocking their shelves with

Chapter Three: The Negative Twenty (-20)

409. As a result, Cinch scored extremely well in the test market and P&G's expectations were high. A national rollout was ordered.

Before P&G could put Cinch into national distribution, Harrell launched a nation-wide promotion, packaging a large refill bottle and a spray bottle together at a substantial price reduction. They flew off of the shelves.

When Cinch hit the market, it performed very poorly against the manufacturer's high expectations. Consumers had stocked up on spray bottles of 409 and a six-month refill. They did not need any more cleaner for a while.

Cinch was removed from the market because sales did not meet expectations.

Harrell understood that every entity, whether it is an organization or an individual, has inherent strengths and weaknesses. Knowing our own strengths and weaknesses is a good start. Also knowing the strengths and weaknesses of the competition can make us invincible, as Harrell demonstrated.

Which leads us to the next tactic that can be used by *–20's* and *21's*.

Step Four: Attack

In 1885, the Westinghouse Gas Company was bringing natural gas to homes and businesses. This required that the Westinghouse Company undertake the Herculean task of installing underground pipes throughout the cities they intended to serve. You know that Mr. Westinghouse had to be a 21 just to consider undertaking the project.

As pipelines were completed, customers were added. The electrical power companies were not too happy about the competition and they put fear in the minds of Westinghouse's potential customers by warning of the possibility of major explosions from the natural gas.

Early one morning there was a tremendous explosion in Sharpsburg, Pennsylvania. The Mill Store, according to the local paper, "blew to atoms" as a result of a natural gas explosion. Fortunately the store was unoccupied at the time and no one was injured. However, the damage to the Westinghouse company and the natural gas industry was significant.

The citizens of Sharpsburg held an "indignation meeting" and most of them vowed to never have a gas appliance in their home or business. If you were Mr. Westinghouse, what would you have done?

Here's what he did: he showed up at the meeting! He agreed to install safety appliances with vents to allow fumes to escape. He offered to make his product even safer than it already was. You see, more people were killed and injured from electrical appliances that year than from gas appliances.

Many of the people at the meeting that night were still afraid of using natural gas appliances as a result of the effective smear campaign from the -20's. At least one person was persuaded by the efforts of Mr. Westinghouse. He went home and wrote in his diary the following words: "My opinion is, inside of two years we will all have it, if we can get it."

> **One catastrophe is not enough to kill a good idea**

The writer was a 21 who recognized the value of the new technology. His faith remained undaunted - one

Chapter Three: The Negative Twenty (-20)

catastrophe was not enough to kill a new idea, he thought. And he should know - he was working his way out of bankruptcy. His own business catastrophe had cost him, his parents, most of his family and many of his friends virtually all of their possessions. His business failure had hurt many people. He did not attend the meeting that night to commiserate with another failure, he attended to offer support and to look for new ways to succeed. His name was H.J. Heinz.

History records and remembers the *21's* who were successful more often than it does the *-20's* who were trying to stop the success from ever happening.

So, was Thomas Watson right or not?

Well, it is true that he built the mainframes that took computers from items of curiosity to tools of necessity. Imagine trying to run a business of any size today without a computer!

One interesting comment that Thomas Watson made was, "I PERCEIVE THERE IS A WORLD MARKET FOR ABOUT FIVE COMPUTERS". What had happened? Watson and his would-be customers were beginning to believe the *-20's* who were saying things like, "Well, there may be some limited applications, but not enough to make the venture a major success."

The company Watson built has been criticized for being slow to embrace the personal computer technology and for allowing Microsoft to determine what the operating system would be. The truth is that the IBM machines set the industry standards, introduced many of the more advanced business applications and further expanded the computer

> **Your idea may be larger than you think...**

53

market. How were they able to succeed in the face of entrepreneurial competition? They did what they believed in and what they did it best. They vowed that nobody would do what they did any better than they did it. You can do the same.

Tom Watson had more than his share of *-20's*. So will you. How will you respond to them?

In this chapter we will discuss the *-20's*, their motives, their attitudes, and their methods. Then we will look at some techniques that have been successful in managing the *-20's*.

> **-20's are stubborn**

The actions of a *-20* spring from a conviction that whatever is being proposed either should not, cannot, or will not be done. A *-20* cannot be budged from this stance. This can work to your advantage if the *-20's* thinking is in your favor, which is rare. If not, the *-20* will oppose you with all of the strength he or she can muster.

Suppose you have an idea for a new business, for attaining a personal goal or for accomplishing something you have never done before. If you are wise, you will seek the advice of those who have done these things in the past. After all, there is little to be gained in reinventing the wheel.

So you go out and begin asking others what they think of your new idea. The *-20's* constitute the largest percentage of the market, so you will see them quickly and often. They will immediately begin telling you why your idea cannot happen.

> **-20's must have a clandestine library somewhere that is filled with "reasons why not"**

Chapter Three: The Negative Twenty (-20)

Want to lose weight? The *-20's* will tell you that a person your age cannot lose weight and keep it off, so why bother? Or they will tell you that losing weight will cause other medical complications and you might as well not subject your body to that stress.

Want to bid for a promotion on the job? Let the word out and the *-20's* will line up to tell you why you'll never make it. "It's a good old boy system", some will say, "if you're not one of the boys, you'll never get the nod." Others will suggest that your bid for the promotion will jeopardize your status in your current position and could actually wind up costing you in the long run. Still others will point out how many more people are significantly more qualified than you and they will wonder aloud how you ever got the idea you could move up.

Tell people you are going to start a business and the *-20's* will quote the statistics of new business failures. Announce that you will be competing in a contest or athletic event and the *-20's* will spout off the odds against your winning.

The goal of the *-20's* is to keep things from happening.

It is interesting, even amusing, to watch the *-20's* in action. Let's say that you and B are both bidding for an opening in your company. The *-20* will tell you all of the reasons why B is the right person for the job: they have more seniority, they have worked numerous positions in the organization and they go to the same church as the decision maker. You don't stand a chance.

While you are mulling that over, the *-20* will go to B and tell them that they cannot possibly be chosen because they have been around too long, they haven't worked any one position long enough and besides, since they attend the same church as the decision maker, others might see their selection for the job as some kind of favoritism.

> *No matter who you are, what you are trying to accomplish and who else might be trying as well, the -20 can find reasons why you cannot, should not and will not achieve your goal.*

> *Paul Coffey was discouraged from becoming a professional hockey player by one of his junior coaches. "He said I couldn't skate, couldn't shoot, couldn't pass the puck and would never play in the NHL", Coffey said. Since then, Coffey has set records for goals, assists and points by a defenseman in a playoff year. And he set these goals in the NHL, the league where he would "never play".*

There are some good points to the *-20's*. For instance the salesperson who calls on a *-20* who likes the salesperson's product has only to take an order. The *-20* is not likely to order from other vendors, and the account is therefore secure. The reason is that the goal of the *-20* is to accomplish nothing. Allowing another salesperson to succeed looks a lot like accomplishment.

This is the type of account preferred by *-20* salespeople. It is easy to handle, involves little change, and presents almost no challenge.

If, on the other hand, your customer is a *-20* who doesn't know about your product, or prefers another brand, you will have a tough sale on your hands. Any presentation or argument made by the salesperson will result in the *-20* buyer telling the salesperson why their product or service cannot,

> ...ignorance
> fear
> jealousy
> laziness

should nor or will not work. (This is the type of prospect a *21* salesman prefers: one that's challenging and risky. More on that later.) The person who puts up unthinking resistance to your new

Chapter Three: The Negative Twenty (-20)

idea may be acting out of ignorance, fear, jealousy, laziness, or any combination of these. In any case, they are a *-20* and their goal is to do nothing, and to allow nothing. The status quo is just fine.

These people are not necessarily sinister or uncaring.

The ignorant *-20* may lack either the intellectual ability or the imagination to grasp your idea. Perhaps he (or she) doesn't have sufficient specialized knowledge in the area in question. Perhaps he's simply kept his head in the sand, instead of staying abreast of advances in the field. For whatever reason, he lacks the knowledge that would prompt him to give your idea a yes vote. And his vote is no.

Therefore when you come across someone who greets your idea with the attitude of a *-20*, be aware that he simply may not know any better. If a person does not understand that something is possible, you will probably have little success convincing him that it will be done.

I paid a call on the vice-president of a large insurance service company. He was a *-20* who had attained his executive position as a result of tenure, seniority, and the help of other Twenties who had made it into the top ranks the same way. I wanted to sell him a telemarketing program for his company, a program for selling over the telephone, which many companies, including his competitors, were using. He showed little interest. I knew that his company was losing money, its stock was down, and layoffs were increasing. My recommendation was designed to stop that trend, and I could not understand why he was not receptive to the idea, I completed my presentation and tried for a close; he wouldn't buy. I answered his questions and tried to pry more questions from him, but he still wouldn't buy.

So I asked a few questions of my own. Didn't he know that his competitors were using telemarketing? In fact, wasn't it this erosion of his business that was causing the problems that his company was having? Wouldn't telemarketing be used in turning that trend around? He answered yes to all of my questions.

"Then why won't you buy?" I asked.

"Because," he explained, "telemarketing would replace all of our field salespeople, and many of them are my friends."

At some point in his past, this *-20* vice-president had been told that telemarketing would eliminate the need for field salespeople. That was not true. If it had been, I would have mentioned it in my proposal since that would certainly have helped to cost justify my recommendation. In fact, the telemarketing program would actually generate more leads for the sales force, and if any change were needed in the number of the sales force, it would be an increase. I overcame his ignorance and eventually closed the sale.

Laziness is the most insidious foe a *21* faces. It may be more apparent in the Twenties. But all of us, even the most driven *21's*, are lazy at heart. While *21's* fight the tendency, Twenties look for the path of least resistance.

> **Laziness is the most insidious foe a *21* faces.**

Imagine this scene. You're sitting at your desk. The telephone messages are piled high. You have three meetings scheduled this week, all of which require hours of preparation. Your boss is waiting for a financial report that was due last Thursday. You couldn't put it together because the figures your assistant handed in were incomplete. Every minute, it seems, your computer beeps to let you know there is another email that needs attention.

Chapter Three: The Negative Twenty (-20)

You get a call from a new staffer in order fulfillment. He has a revolutionary plan for streamlining packaging and shipping procedures. He figures that it would cost X dollars and could be implemented by the end of next year. He's asking for your input. You promise to think about it and call him back. You go back to your own problems. The revolutionary packing and shipping plan? It might work and it might not. It would require months of testing and a big investment. Of course, you look after the budgets, and the guy can't move without your support. But who wants to think about this right now? You don't have the time and you don't have the energy. You know that he's going to call you back for an answer. What's the fastest, easiest way to take care of the matter? Reject the plan. Tell him the time isn't right. You dash off a memo to that effect and put it in the out box. Problem disposed of. Too bad for him.

Had you been so inclined, you could have given the fellow's plan more consideration. You could have discovered it to be a fine plan, even a brilliant one. But that kind of serious consideration would have required time, thought, maybe even a little research. You didn't want to make the effort. Most people in the same situation would act the same way, you rationalize to yourself. You're right. Most people do.

The most potent motivator for the *-20* is fear. Fear is the strongest motivator for most of us, and *-20's* are no different. The two things that a *-20* fears most are change and commitment. There is the fear that change will, somehow, lead to ruin. Life as we know it, with all of its comfortable ruts, ends whenever there is change. Some people cannot handle that: they are the *-20's*.

Fear is the most potent motivator for the –20's

In a business environment, an idea for change means new procedures, new responsibilities, an upset in the routine. Changes aimed at improving efficiency often mean more automation or computerization. People who will be affected by your proposed change perceive that, at the very least, they may have to switch off the automatic pilot and actually think about their jobs again. At worst, their jobs may become less important or unnecessary. No wonder their first reaction is tinged with fear.

In our personal lives, change creates the potential for unsettling events. When we think about any of the changes that might come into our lives, we begin to play the mental "what if" game. What if the change causes me to lose respect among my friends or family? What if I cannot manage the change and it results in a negative economic or other downfall? What if my spouse changes jobs? Will I see more or less of them? Will I be required to take on additional responsibilities?

The opposite of fear is faith. The *-20* operates out of fear, the *21* operates out of faith.

> *The opposite of fear is faith*

The *-20* fears commitment because, all too often, commitment requires offensive (as opposed to defensive) action. *-20's* are in the habit of reacting, not acting. If you study the old attitudes to which the *-20's* cling, you will see that they are defensive attitudes. Attitudes like: "Things are going along fine just as they are." and "You can't teach an old dog new tricks." They do not require any assertive or aggressive action but instead are used to defend a lack of action.

Fear of change and fear of commitment can compel *-20's* to overcome their laziness and to resist any change or threat with tremendous stamina. Whenever a scared *-20* senses that a change is in the offing, he or she will expend whatever effort is necessary to block the change. The *-20's* will even spend more energy trying to stop something from happening than it would take to make the new idea happen. It is unlikely that you will ever win a round with a truly frightened *-20*. Most of them can go the distance and hardly work up a sweat.

Chapter Three: The Negative Twenty (-20)

Maybe you see some of yourself in this discussion of the motives of the *-20's*. At least you can begin to understand why they act as they do. Keep in mind that everyone has the potential to be a *20* and most people have the potential to be a *21*. The difference is a matter of attitude.

To kill a new idea, *-20's* favor two very powerful and lethal responses that can be applied in almost any situation:

RESPONSE NUMBER 1: It's been done.

RESPONSE NUMBER 2: Don't mess with success.

Other Twenties will accept either response and drop the new idea. They are easily discouraged and accept the first obstacle as the dead end. But *21's* will persevere until they ACHIEVE THEIR GOAL, aware that the stock response from the *-20* is really only an obstacle. *-20's* use these responses because they are usually successful: *-20's* accept them at face value, *+20's* allow themselves to be easily discouraged, and many would-be *21's* will give in to the persistent application of Responses 1 and 2. Only a true *21* can survive a *-20* who understands the power of "It's been done" or "Don't mess with success."

The premise behind Response Number 1, "It's been done," is that, since it has been done, there is no reason to try it again. If it was tried once before and failed, there is no reason to try it again because it will just fail again. If it was a success, there is no reason to try it again because it would just be a duplicate, me-too endeavor. The astute *-20* can always produce an example from the past that resembles, at least to some degree, the new idea at hand.

The other line, "Don't mess with success," sometimes known as, "If it ain't broke, don't fix it" is used to maintain the status quo. According to too

> **Don't mess with success.
> If it ain't broke, don't fix it.**

many *-20's*, nothing should ever be attempted that might affect the way things are presently being done. After all, the fact that we are doing something today should attest to the validity of the method being used. If it wasn't the right way to do something, we wouldn't be doing it. As long as the *-20* is able to sell this line of thinking, he succeeds in discouraging change.

Suppose the idea on the table is to begin a new advertising campaign. The *-20's* can invoke either response. Response Number 1 can be used to show that previous ad campaigns either produced all the results that were needed or produced little. Either way, a new campaign is not needed. Response Number 2 could be brought in to justify leaving the present ad campaign in place.

If the *21* introduces the idea of writing a motivational book, Response Number 1 is the vehicle for rejection. The *-20* will do a mental data dump and tell the *21* about the large number of books that are submitted to publishers every year and subsequently fail. Well-versed *-20's* have good memories for negative statistics. They have total recall when "no" responses are involved and no recollection when "yes" reasons are needed. If the *21* persists with reasons why his or her book can overcome the odds, the *-20* will do a turnabout. The *-20* will then admit that, yes, a number of good motivational books have overcome the odds and made it into print. In fact, so many have been published that now the market is saturated and there is no need for any more motivational books. Substitute any other adjective for "motivational", such as computer, photography, mathematics, or travel books and you'll see how universal the *-20's* invalid objection can be.

> **Well-versed *-20's* have good memories for negative statistics.**

In 1966 I met a very old man with one of the most heartbreaking stories about succumbing to the responses of the Twenties. He told

Chapter Three: The Negative Twenty (-20)

me that when he was at the beginning of his career, an entrepreneur approached him, offering to exchange a partnership in his new business for three thousand dollars. The entrepreneur wanted to produce and market a new nonalcoholic drink that had the ability to refresh and stimulate people after physical exertion.

The old man had asked several people what they thought about the entrepreneur's idea. Some said, "It's been done." There were numerous products of every description already available including quinine water and sarsaparilla. Others reminded him that most new products fail. Still others tried to convince the man that he should not mess with success. His money was earning interest in the bank and he already had a good job. The man I was talking to turned down the offer from the entrepreneur. The entrepreneur's name: Asa Candler; his drink: Coca-Cola, "The Pause That Refreshes."

A *-20* might also use a company rule or the latest commandment from upper management to stop you in your tracks. If you're handed this kind of a quick no, you may wonder why someone would dismiss an idea without even thinking it through, and then back up his position with blanket rules or instructions that have nothing to do with the specific situation you want to see changed. When that happens, you may want to consider the following.

When the *-20* heard your idea, he did, just for a moment, entertain the possibility of pursuing it. He put himself into your shoes. But he did not think of what would happen if someone else tried to push it through, he thought of what would happen if he himself made the attempt. And being a pessimist and a *-20*, he knew that he would

> Don't take the noise of the *20* too seriously; they typically only consider what would happen to them if *they* tried what you are suggesting.

fail, and jumped to the quick conclusion that <u>anyone's</u> attempt would fail. And so by advising you to abandon your idea, he thinks that he's sparing you unnecessary effort and disappointment.

A rule or an instruction from higher up provides him with a safe and easy out. After all, the *-20* didn't make the rule that your innovative plan might violate, and he takes no responsibility for that rule. In discouraging a possible infraction, he's simply following orders. Nobody can fault him for that, he thinks.

> **A 20 can interpret almost any rule in a way that will make it a tool for them.**

Your best bet is to go to the source of the rule or the instruction. What is the reason behind the rule? What were the circumstances that caused your organization to make it in the first place? The chances are that the company got burned because of an unfortunate course of action, and the policy was laid down to avoid the same mistake and the same results. If you can show that your plan will produce better results, you have a powerful argument to use against *-20's* who have a detailed knowledge of the rulebook.

If you have ever played the game "Gossip", you know how messages can change as they pass from one person to another. The game involves people sitting in a circle. Someone says something to the person next to them who then passes the information to the person next to them. The message continues around the circle until the last person tells what they heard. There is typically a lot of difference in the original and final versions of the message.

The same thing happens in the corporate world. The senior executives find it necessary to issue an edict because of some unfavorable event. As the message is passed down to the troops, it tends to change with each telling, usually to the benefit of the

Chapter Three: The Negative Twenty (-20)

speaker. It is human nature to slant a story to the benefit of the one telling the story.

Find out what the real rules are. Find out what

Find out what the *real* rules are

basis the *-20* is using to disparage your idea and then move forward.

Sometimes the *-20* is simply misinterpreting the instructions that he's received. For instance, when the President of the company said, "We must be careful with all fourth quarter expenditures," the *-20* department head heard: "Don't spend any money in the fourth quarter." So when you take your idea to this department, one of the middle managers feels perfectly confident in telling you, "The president has said that we can't spend any money on new projects right now."

I have learned through experience to verify such quotes at the horse's mouth. I once presented a business case to my organization, A.T.& T, that showed how it could generate $3 million in revenue over an eighteen-month period with an investment of $150,000. This would be accomplished by my company's providing a new service to our business customers that had a toll-free 800 telephone number. This service would identify callers to the toll-free number by region and provide demographic information about them. I erroneously thought that it would be an easy sale. After all, a twenty - to - one payback is a good return.

As I moved through the *-20's*, I came against the same response again and again: "The president won't allow us to produce any system that requires nonstandard equipment." Now, can you imagine the president of a multimillion-dollar company refusing a solid business case like this one because of a technicality? The *-20's* thought they were secure because nobody would ever contact the *president*. I did, and I sold the project. It generated revenues higher than our expectations, and continued to do so even after I left the company.

It eventually led to a product now known as Caller ID. Did I invent Caller ID? No more than Al Gore invented the Internet. What I did was to listen to my customer. He told me that having that information would be of tremendous value to him. I simply asked, "How valuable?" and he answered, "$3 million".

At the same time, other AT&T Account Executives like me were hearing the same thing from their customers. Their customers also saw value in having that information. So, they took the idea back inside AT&T just as I did. They heard all of the excuses from the *20's* and bought into them. I was either too stupid or too stubborn to buy into the "no".

The persistent *21* will push and ask why their plan can't/shouldn't/won't be done.

Another tactic you will observe in the *-20's* is what I call the Absolute Rule. Listen for "Absolutes". They are one of the most overt indicators that you are communicating with a *20*.

THERE ARE NO ABSOLUTES IN LIFE

There are no absolutes in life, yet the *-20's* will use them as if they were law. They will say things like "Everybody knows that...", "Nobody will ever ...", "There has never been and will never be ..." There are no absolutes. When you hear an absolute being used to justify a position, imagine you are hearing an alarm bell. Is there a base of knowledge that everyone has? Is there a universal truth that everyone agrees to? I don't think so.

Chapter Three: The Negative Twenty (-20)

When confronted by a *-20*, you may be tempted to ask what the basis is for their rejecting your idea. If they lack a more valid sounding one, they will choose one of the absolute reasons: Everybody, Nobody, etc.

If the one-on-one discouragement fails, the *-20* will resort to a public forum: the conference room, the boardroom, or even a social event. The *-20* is not above taking pot shots at the *21* or attempting to humiliate the *21* in front of others. When their backs are up against the wall, the *-20's* can be vicious.

> **If the one-on-one discouragement fails, the next step is a public forum**

After the defeat of Germany in World War Two, leading automobile executives from around the world visited the plant where the Volkswagen Beetle was being produced. The task force included the current president of the Ford Motor Company. His assessment of the Beetle was that it was worthless and that the American people would never buy it. His British counterpart said, "The Volkswagen does not meet the fundamental technical requirements of a motor car."

Later Ford would launch the most comprehensive market research ever that was focused on designing and building the perfect American automobile. The end result was the Edsel, a name that has become synonymous with failure. The British continued to build their brand of automobiles that suffered from a reputation of unreliability.

Fifty years after the tour of the Volkswagen plant and thirty years after the last Edsel rolled off of the assembly line, the Beetle was still selling well in the United States. After a lull of a couple of decades when the car was only selling well in forty-

plus countries, it made a comeback in the United States. You just cannot keep a good *21* or their product down.

An interesting thing happens when the *21* succeeds: the *20* takes credit for the success that they had originally opposed. This seemingly illogical event occurs when everything goes well. *21's* succeed in spite of, not because of, the actions of the *-20's*. But once the

> **20's will attempt to take credit for the success they initially opposed**

success is complete, the *-20* steps in to receive some of the accolades. *-20's* do this for two reasons: to maintain a feel for what the *21* is doing, and to maintain whatever existing control the *-20* has in the organization or situation. The *21's* allow the *-20* to share in the credit partly to help permanently neutralize them and partly out of an optimistic attitude that the *-20* will see the light.

If the *21* is unwilling to share the limelight with the *-20*, the *-20* will continue to work against him. Some *-20's* have a strong enough power base to take credit for the success anyway.

Robert Woodruff, the Chairman of Coca Cola, was a consummate *21*. He once said, "It is amazing what you can accomplish if you

> **"It is amazing what you can accomplish if you don't care who gets the credit."** - Robert Woodruff

don't care who gets the credit." He was a legendary philanthropist and many of his contributions were done anonymously. Decades after his death the stories are still being uncovered about people he helped anonymously.

21's will allow Twenties, even *-20's* to steal some of the limelight. The *21's* think that maybe enough exposure to positive events will

Chapter Three: The Negative Twenty (-20)

make the *-20's* a little more amenable to new ideas in the future. It rarely works but *21's* are a hopelessly optimistic lot.

You should always be aware of where you are in the corporation and where the *-20's* are. If you are the CEO, you should understand where the *-20's* are, since they are undermining your organization. If you are on your way to the top, learn where the *-20's* are who will try to trip you up or stop you. If you are anywhere in the organization, take a long look at the front office. Are there *-20's* at the top? Look for the telltale signs:

- Does your company experiment with new policies and procedures, or is business conducted in the same old way from season to season?
- Does it take advantage of new technologies and the latest in office automation equipment?
- Is it constantly on the lookout for new markets for its products or services, and new ways to reach those markets, or does it rely on long-established accounts and familiar outlets to keep itself going?
- Do you have to fill out ten forms to get anything accomplished, and do those forms look as if they haven't been revised in a decade?

Time worn procedures, obsolete equipment and facilities, and lots of red tape are the marks of an organization dominated by *-20's*. If this is the case, you may have a difficult time overcoming the blocking tactics of low-level *-20's*.

I took the position of sales manager for an account that was performing badly. The customer did not like our company, its products or its people. I was given the position to try and correct the situation and was told by a great many Twenties that it could not be done. My first move was to interview every member of my organization. The last salesman was a *-20* and a newly hired salesman was a *-20*. Both of these people had transferred into sales from other departments, both had more seniority with the company than I did, and both were able to offer solid sounding reasons why things could not, should not or would not be done. They would offer that the customer had rejected similar proposals in the past, that our solution was not in the customer's best interest, or that the customer had decided to go with the competition.

These gentlemen would sit in sales meetings and shoot down every idea for managing the account. They would occasionally offer suggestions (at my insistence), and their new ideas were always reruns of the ways things had been done in the past - yesterday's ideas.

They accomplished little. On several occasions, customers would call in to place an order, to give us some business, only to have one of the *-20's* answer the phone and tell the customer, "It's not my job." Fortunately, the customer would have the patience to call me up and chew me out but allow us to retain the sale.

I tried to motivate these two, but found that the account couldn't wait for improvement, that changes were needed immediately, and so they were sent to other departments. Each of them received an evaluation before leaving and both were disappointed with the marks they received. Since AT&T had more than it's share of Twenties, it was not difficult to find another position for each of them; had the company been controlled by *21's* these two would never have been there in the first place.

I replaced these gentlemen with *21's*, and a year later the revenue from this account had *doubled*, customer rapport was at an all-time high, and the account team was leading all others in results. Sometimes just a few *-20's* or a few *21's* can make all the difference.

Chapter Three: The Negative Twenty (-20)

As you try to make any project happen, you will encounter the *-20's*. Your first thought may be to try to figure out a way to eliminate them altogether. Giving in to that temptation can be risky. In a sizable organization, the Twenties have the strength of numbers. You never know how much support a *-20* has, and you may be surprised to see who comes forth to rescue him or her. On the other hand, you can't afford to have a *-20* on your side either; that's like trying to carry a sack of potatoes in a marathon race. You have a large enough challenge ahead of you without adding unnecessary encumbrances.

One way to deal with *-20's* is to try to neutralize them. *-20's* will rarely support your cause for change, but maybe you will succeed in at least moving them out of the way. For instance, if your impossible goal was to fly across the Atlantic in a hot-air balloon, you would never convince a *-20* to climb into the gondola with you. You might, however, talk him into letting go of the mooring ropes.

There is an art to neutralizing *-20's*, and you will become more proficient at managing them with practice. The first step is to determine what motivates a particular *-20*. If you don't know, just ask. *-20's* are usually eager to tell you why they believe something cannot, should not or will not be done.

I find that one of the best ways to neutralize the *-20* is to appear to agree with him. Assure them that you understand their point of view, and that you will be the clown on stage making the blunders. Actually, your goal is pure success, but the *-20* will not move aside until you acknowledge, at least to them, that you agree with their assessment of probable failure. At this point, the pride of the *-20* is intact, and even though they have no intention of trying to join you, they are willing to step aside and give you enough rope to hang yourself.

If you find that a *-20* is motivated by fear, you may have more success than you would in the previous situation. Alleviate that person's fears by showing them that their fears are unfounded (that the individual will not be affected by your project). Let them know you are willing to take the heat and they may back away and let you have your way. *-20's* delight in watching a *21* make a fool out of himself - it solidifies their philosophy.

In cases where the *-20* is motivated by ignorance, take a shot at educating him as I educated the insurance company vice-president about telemarketing. In the section on *21's* later in this book, you will learn that some Twenties are really *21's* who just need a push. I usually think it's worthwhile to attempt to awaken the *21* inside the *20* whenever possible. Find out why the *-20* believes he knows that something cannot be done, and try to teach him the truth. Tell the *-20* what you intend to do, how you intend to do it, and what you expect to accomplish. This shows that you have thought through your plan and know where you're going. *-20's* rarely do any planning, so quite often just seeing a plan of action shakes a *-20* into believing that there may be a better way of doing things.

Expect the *-20's*. Learn to recognize them, and learn to manage them. You can use your plan to neutralize some of them and maybe even change some of them. The remainder will have to be worked around.

Also, expect the *21's*. Read the next chapter on the *+20's*, and then we'll discuss a more exciting subject: the *21's*.

Chapter Four

The Positive Twenty (+20)

There is a slippery critter in your life. A master of charade and disguise, this chameleon can take on the appearance of a *21*, your best advocate and an endorser of your ideas. Meanwhile, they will do all that they can to keep you from accomplishing anything. Their goal is the same as the *-20*, making nothing happen. They take a positive approach to keeping things from happening so I call them the Positive Twenties (*+20's*). They are difficult to identify because they closely resemble a *21*, but their accomplishments are the same as those of a *-20*. The *+20* openly encourages you, agrees that there is merit in your idea, even offers to help and yet continues to work against whatever you are trying to accomplish.

Masters of procrastination, the *+20's* can readily give you a solid reason why your idea is good and *should be done* - tomorrow. Adherents of the tried - and - true, they will whole heartedly endorse your idea as one that needs to be done - a little differently than you are suggesting (you know, a lot more like the way we are already doing things). Don't spend much time with the *+20's*. It is usually wasted. Unfortunately, the only way to know for sure that individuals are *+20's* is to allow them to run their course. You will know the *+20's* by their fruits. Though they talk a good game, when all is said and done, a lot gets said and nothing gets done. Since these people are not up front about their intent to block your progress as the *-20's* are, it can sometimes take a long time to distinguish a *+20* from a *21*.

Even so, there are a few very suspicious signs that may help you sniff out a *+20*. I'm sure there are people in your life who sometimes make you wonder. You see them from day to day. They are agreeable, seem to fit in well and to command respect. They may appear to be go-getters, look important, and seem busy, and they don't have any huge flops attached to their names. But you can't figure out what it is they actually do. When you see these people, you're probably looking at *+20's*.

Because *+20's* so often resemble *21's*, they can rise quite high in the organization. They do not necessarily work or earn their way up, but they are often able to go surprisingly far. To understand how this occurs, take a look at the promotion process in large corporations. Whenever there is a vacancy at any level, people will begin to line up for the job. If the person who is responsible for selecting the person is a *20*, then the position is likely to be filled by a *20*. You understand that *20's* do not enjoy working around *21's* and will use their influence to put one of their own in the slot. So do not be surprised if you happen to find one or more *+20's* on Mahogany Row. When you think about it, it makes sense. Here is a person who never says no but never disturbs the status quo. Such an incredible balancing act deserves all the perks of the executive suite.

+20's also show up as committee chairpersons and even presidents of civic organizations. They are elected by other *20's*, both *+20's* and *-20's*, so that the group will sound like it is progressive without ever having to actually try anything.

Chapter Four: The Positive Twenty (+20)

Congress is a prime example of *+20's* at work. During their respective campaigns, the politicians gave grand speeches about how they will change things for the better. Two or four years later, they are making the same promises (unless others are more popular) while offering reasons and excuses for not achieving these same goals during their last tenure. Whatever it takes to win the race will be promised; once in the seat the game is to maintain the status quo.

> **Congress is a prime example of +20's at "work"**

The quality that *+20's* and *21's* seem to share is enthusiasm. The quality that separates the one group from the other is accomplishment. *+20's* don't accomplish, not because they aren't as able as *21's*, but because they are afraid to try. To try is to risk failure, and *+20's* fear failure more than they desire success.

Failure sticks. *20's* will remember the failures even if they forget the successes. *20's* will remind one another that a certain *21* failed at a certain endeavor whenever they need reasons for not doing something.

People in the United States worship winners and loathe failures. We have a low tolerance for the lack of success at anything. Therefore, for many people, it is better not to try than to try and fail. *+20's* always believe themselves to be winners because, by their definition, they never fail. To them, avoidance of failure equals success.

+20's are considered to be progressive because they openly endorse new and innovative ideas. As long as they are not forced to act on these ideas and run the risk of failure, then they get along fine. They bask in the reflection of other people's successes. After all, they

> **Once an idea succeeds, the +20 can say they were behind the idea from the beginning**

were one of the ones who were endorsing the idea originally. Never

75

mind that they threw up countless roadblocks and did all they could to stop the new idea from becoming reality. Once someone succeeds, the *+20* can say they were behind the idea from the beginning.

Years ago a friend of mine opened a recreational vehicle dealership. He had already succeeded at a couple of other ventures and could have retired at the age of forty-five. But like most entrepreneurs, he had to have something going. A few months after he began his business, there was an embargo imposed on Arab oil imports and gasoline prices reached an all-time high. Almost everyone in the RV business including my friend lost everything.

One day he asked me why so many people thought he was a failure. He noted that six months earlier these same people could not say enough nice things about him. Now, it seemed, he was treated as if he had the plague. *20's* think that failure is contagious and so avoid those who are afflicted with it. My friend could not understand how the people could call him a failure when they had *never even tried.*

The last time I saw him he was on his way to making another million dollars in the sporting goods market. The same people who had said that he was a failure were now saying they "always knew he would make it".

Try to find a company that does not consider itself to be progressive. In fact, try to find a manager who does not

Most people consider themselves to be progressive

think of himself or herself as innovative. The *+20's* think of themselves this way, after all, and are quick to point out that they have made changes in the way things are being done.

Chapter Four: The Positive Twenty (+20)

Several years ago I interviewed the manager of a collection bureau whose operation was losing money for the fifth consecutive year. I was trying to sell him a system that would automate his entire collections process, which was manual at the time. The manual shuffling of paper was astounding. I brought in a systems analyst to look at the situation, and she threw up her hands in despair. We calculated that 80 percent of the energies of the staff of that office were expended on locating pieces of paper. The employees could not be more productive because they could not find the work they needed to do without several hours' search for a single sheet of paper.

My recommendation would eliminate 25 percent of the manager's work force, increase his volume by 30 percent, and improve his bottom line by nearly 48 percent. He indicated that he had already solved the problem by rearranging the desks. He surmised that if the paper flow was reduced in distance (not in function), then each piece of paper would be easier to find. This is the way the *+20* thinks. He could make "significant changes" as evidenced by the new furniture arrangement, without having to change the fundamental way things were being done.

My approach would eliminate enough labor-intensive functions to eliminate some of the desks. Another of my objectives was to put this company in the black. Moving desks around wasn't going to do it. The point is that this *+20* manager considered himself progressive and his feeble effort to solve the problem perfectly sufficient. He attempted to thwart my efforts without thoroughly evaluating my idea.

Want to know the outcome? We both lost. I went around this branch manager and my study and my business case to the corporate headquarters. While I managed to convince many of the players, I did not overcome the company's basic philosophy of letting the branch manager have the ultimate responsibility. I lost the sale. A few weeks later, the branch manager was replaced. I wish I had been able to recognize him as a *+20*.

+20's live in a fascinating world all their own. I call it "life in the middle lane." They stay out of the fast lane, where the *21's* are found zipping along. They also avoid the slow lane, which belongs to the *-20's*. Life in the middle lane is a series of experiences that involve little more than moving from point A to point B, passing enough people along the way to appear successful. Anyone who passes in the fast lane is considered by the *+20* to be reckless and headed for disaster (failure). The *+20* considers those in the slow lane to be the norm and thinks he is surpassing the average person.

> **+20's live in a fascinating world of their own**

In other words, the *+20's* philosophy is, "I'm faster than the slow and slower than the reckless". Try to argue with that!

Once you understand the perspective of the *+20's*, it becomes easier to understand the rationale behind their behavior. After all, they *are* making progress: nice, safe progress. Usually their progress is mandatory progress: changes that are forced on them. If they fail to address this change, they will be subjected to some penalty. Once the change is obviously inevitable and the *+20* has run out of alternatives, they will capitulate to the change.

> **Once you understand the +20's, you will be better able to manage them**

For instance, the *+20's* were the ones to decry the use of pocket calculators. They preferred the tried and true slide rule. Once slide rules were no longer being manufactured, were more expensive than calculators and were proven to be slower and less accurate, then the

Chapter Four: The Positive Twenty (+20)

+20's made the change. They take the same approach to any new technology including PC's, PDA's, MP3 players, etc.

+20's will shop at the same store on the same day of the week and buy the same products until the store closes or stops carrying the product. Then, with no other options before them, the *+20* will make a change.

Probably the easiest and quickest way to sort out the *-20's*, *+20's*, and *21's* in a crowd is to give each of them an automobile. The *-20* will take the usual route home, sticking to the slow lane. If any obstacle should get in his way, the *-20* will stop until it is cleared. The *-20* will also be oblivious to the fact that everyone else is making better time than he is. He will ignore any available detour because it is untried ground.

> The *+20*, as we have discussed, will take the middle lane: faster than his perception of the average, slower than his perception of the reckless.

The *21* will enter the freeway and use *any* lane to reach his or her goal. When speed is necessary, the *21* will not hesitate to use the fast lane. After all, there will not be any *20's* there to obstruct his passage. However, the shrewdest of the *21's* know that, to be successful, there are times when the smartest thing to do is to act like a *20* and take the middle or even the slow lane. The *21* is not afraid to maneuver to move around the obstacles in order to achieve his goals.

The *+20* has many success stories to relate. This is one reason he seems to closely resemble a *21*. These success stories concern those conquests in the middle lane. The *+20* considers passing a poor performer to be a successful achievement, just as he considers avoiding failure to be synonymous with success. To state it simply, the *+20* ignores the successes of those ahead of him and revels in the failures of those behind him.

Thomas Edison was one of the most perplexing *+20's*. That's right Thomas Edison. He accomplished many things, held many patents and is generally credited with being the inventor of many useful machines including the phonograph and the dictograph. However, if it weren't his idea, one that he had conceived and pushed, he would become the creator's *+20*. He was even a *+20* for a few of his own creations.

> **Remarkably, Thomas Edison was a +20 on many occasions**

Here are some of his *+20* comments. *"The aero plane will never be of any commercial use, and neither will the phonograph. They both have uses as amusing pastimes, but no commercial value. Talking pictures will never make it; people prefer the silent movies. Steam engines will not be replaced by internal combustion engines. Steam engines are better and stronger."*

In one very public, celebrated and nearly forgotten case, Edison was trying to convince the general public and public officials that D.C. current was the only type of electricity that would be usable, not the A.C. current you have in your home. Obviously Edison lost this battle, but he spent a small fortune and much of his energy to try to kill Mr. Westinghouse's alternating current system. Edison even went so far as to speak in favor of the electric chair, a device that relied on the competitive A.C. current. The reason was that he wanted people to see that A.C. current was potentially lethal.

Of course, there is one twist here: Edison had invested heavily in D.C. lamps, motors and other products. A.C. current would not make him any money, D.C. current would. Sometimes there is method behind the madness of the *20's*.

Chapter Four: The Positive Twenty (+20)

Another arena where *+20's* reveal themselves is in sports. Every year one team ends up on top - not two teams, one team. Since athletics are so competitive, there is an unusually high percentage of *21's* around locker rooms. The winning team is usually the one with the most *21's*, but even the losing teams will have their share of them. Teams coached by *20's* or composed of *20's* will end their season close to the bottom of the heap.

The *+20's* will end their season as also-rans, but you would never know it to hear them talk. *+20's* can tell you about all the points they scored and about how much better they are than teams that they defeated. Any discussion about the teams to whom they lost is usually short and punctuated with remarks about how the other team played the game recklessly and untraditionally or how the other team just got lucky.

> **There is only one first place team**

Even losing teams will have their stories of victories, but only one team will have the championship. One thing that the *+20's* never seem to understand is that it does no good to be the number one quarterback on the last-place team - you still don't go to the Superbowl.

Many people ask me: "What's wrong with mediocrity?" *+20's* have their share of successes and they aren't suffering from ulcers, overexertion, or stress, right?

> **So, what's wrong with mediocrity? Stress!**

Wrong. *+20's* spend a lot of energy and wind up with their share of tension as a result of trying to appear to be better than the worst. They also create pressure for themselves whenever they watch a *21* try to achieve the impossible. The *+20* holds his breath, hoping that the **21** will fail, because success for the **+20** is the failure of a **21**. I'll never understand why anyone would go through so much for mediocrity, when only a little more energy would bring stardom.

+20's loathe the successes of the **21's**, and it is this loathing that creates stress for the **+20**. I like to say that the best way for a **+20** to get unstressed is to take his loathes off.

You are probably reading this book because you want to achieve, because you want to be a success. Understand what real success is before you go after it.

+20's are in the magic category between success and failure. They are really neither. **+20's** never feel the exhilaration associated with true success nor do they experience the agony of failure. And while their apparent successes would lead you to believe that their overall performance was one of achievement, remember that they still are not bringing home the pennant. If you are content with "almost," then you don't need to waste your time reading the rest of this book.

> **If you never expect anything, you'll never be disappointed**

One of the mottoes of the **+20** is: If you never expect anything, you'll never be disappointed.

Do you remember when the first sub-four-minute mile was run? At one time it was considered a physical impossibility to run a mile in less than four minutes. Some of the best doctors, trainers, and coaches agreed that no human could endure the strain that such an effort would put on the body. Somewhere along the line, an athlete named Roger Bannister did not get the word. In 1954 he ran a mile in three minutes and fifty-nine seconds. The magic of the three minute mile had been achieved and from then on the **+20's** sought to match Bannister's achievement. The **21's** sought to better it.

Chapter Four: The Positive Twenty (+20)

Several years ago in a college track meet in Orange County, California, a young athlete ran a mile in less than four minutes and no one said anything to him. Why? He came in fourth and we only acknowledge the first three runners. What used to be good enough and most significant enough that it became a part of history is no longer good enough for amateur competition. If someone says, "Four Minute Mile", we think of Roger Bannister. If they say, "Roger Bannister", we think of breaking the four-minute mile. Today, breaking the four-minute mile is not special.

All over the world there are runners who are training for the mile run. The *+20's* are training to break the four-minute mark, not to win the race. They will lose the race and not be disappointed because they have done what few have done - they broke the mythical barrier. The *21's* are training to win the race. They will also break the four-minute mark, win the race, and not be disappointed. Following the race, the *+20's* will tell about the runners they passed and boast of their speed. The *21's* will wear their ribbons and have their names recorded in the record books. That's the difference.

+20's are the absolute nemesis of salespeople. The *+20* is that proverbial customer who keeps encouraging the salesperson right up to the signing of the contract, and then balks. The *+20* tells you on your first visit that he has already talked to his boss about the need for your product. As you make your initial presentation, he notes that your product is exactly what he needs, just as he told

+20's are the nemesis of salespeople

the boss. Of course, there is no need for you to talk to the boss, since he already has the manager's ear.

When you think you've done enough selling and the time is right to close the deal, the **+20** will begin to give you reasons why he will not be able to sign today, but may be able to - tomorrow.

I used to wonder why **+20's** did this. Some of them just don't like to say no. I guess they think it will hurt the salesperson's feelings. So instead they just string the salesperson along until he or she gives up. Most likely, though, the **+20** assumes that the salesperson is just as much a **+20** as they are; that he or she doesn't really expect to actually make the sale and will go away quietly without demanding a decision. We like to think that everyone is like us, don't we?

Always remember, in most cases the salesperson needs the customer more than the customer needs the salesperson. To sell to a **+20**, you must reverse that. Whether you are selling a product, an idea or a project, the **+20** is the buyer and you are the seller. Here is how to work around the **+20**.

There's a pattern the **+20's** follow when they are about to stall. The first maneuver is to maintain their facade of being the decision maker. Through continued reassurances, they will make it clear that the decision rest with them. They will try to stall until you lose interest so that they can accuse you of giving up. This keeps them from having to make a decision, which they are not likely to do anyway.

How to sell to the +20

As you push for decisive action, a **+20** will begin interjecting little comments about having to consult with upper management, the committee or their partner. He is the decision maker, he reaffirms, but he has to "run the whole thing by headquarters - just a formality." **+20's** will request numerous proposals, each one only slightly different from the first. Their reasoning will be that they are trying to make your recommendation palatable to the brass, the

Chapter Four: The Positive Twenty (+20)

committee members or other members of the team. They are there to help you. They know what others expect and they are only trying to maximize your chance of success. At some point you will tire of this and push for a close. *+20's* will either turn you down or - and this happens most frequently - move on to maneuver number two.

The second maneuver is comical because the *+20's* take it so seriously. I call it the "*+20's* Martyr Performance". The point of the *+20's* Martyr Performance is to place the blame for a final, delayed "no" on someone else. The *+20* is still positive, but seems to suffer right along with you, like a martyr. This person was "really on your side," and now you are both defeated, or so the *+20* would have you believe. Actually,

> **Once you and the +20 fail to achieve anything, they have succeeded**

he has succeeded in achieving his goal of having nothing happen.

This is where the *+20* expects the issue to stop. The *21*, of course, is still in hot pursuit of his objective. It is not uncommon at this point for the *+20* to turn into a *-20*. He is convinced that the project cannot and/or should not be done and will try to convince you of the same thing. This newly emerged *-20* will be extremely tough to handle, because he already has every detail of your idea and knows any weaknesses. In addition, he may have already mustered support for his position of opposition. Once the *+20* succumbs to the *-20's* at the top, it behooves him to align himself with them.

There was a *21* working for a large insurance company as a property design and procurement manager. Her job was to design the office space needed for different areas, locate suitable parcels of property, and negotiate the sale or lease of those properties. Her name was Martha, and her partner in that particular group was a *+20* named Jim. Jim had taught Martha the ropes and thought he had her well indoctrinated in the ways of the *20's*.

As time wore on, Martha distinguished herself as a top-notch negotiator and an able designer. Many of her ideas were adopted, but as they veered further and further from the tried-and-true, she met with more and more rejection, both from Jim and from others in the company. Her goal was to change the public's perception of the corporation by improving the appearance of the local offices located all over the country. Martha was also a student of human sciences and understood the impact that an environment has on an individual's performance. She used that knowledge to improve productivity in the offices she designed.

Martha was well respected throughout the company and was moved up in management. Because of this, Jim the *+20*, appeared to support her even though he was anything but supportive behind her back. He had two reasons for this charade. One was that if her ideas were accepted, he wanted to be a part of them so that he would know what was going on in his own department and share in the glory. The other was that he wanted to stop anything Martha might accomplish that would threaten the status quo. Over coffee in the headquarters cafeteria, he would openly voice his concern to his buddies about the "little girl" and her strange ideas. But when he was alone with her, he readily endorsed her concept and offered to speak to his old buddies in the executive suite.

If you have the impression that the *+20* here may have felt that this young upstart threatened his position, your impression is probably correct.

This particular corporation was dominated by *20's* and strictly adhered to old-line, conservative business principles. There were few risk-takers, and the management philosophy and operating procedures hadn't changed much in decades.

Martha, for all of her strong *21* characteristics, was fighting a situation where the ultimate decision makers were *20's*. Jim would

Chapter Four: The Positive Twenty (+20)

tell her that he could sell any decision from their department. In fact, he could sell it only if he wanted to and only if the decision did not radically depart from the norm. Jim was always a *+20* until the brass put pressure on him and turned him into a conforming *-20*. In corporations headed by *20's*, the manager with aspirations knows when it's okay to be a *+20* and when it's smart to be a *-20*. In corporations headed by *20's*, the manager with aspirations knows when it's okay to be a *+20* and when it's smart to be a *-20*.

One day Martha and I were discussing her situation. I already knew most of the details, since I was representing a vendor that wanted to sell the latest in electronic communications equipment to her corporation. My role as salesman for new location equipment overlapped with her responsibility as designer and procurer of new locations. We had both suffered the same frustrations in trying to sell our ideas inside this corporation.

I began explaining The Theory of *21* to her, and it was as if a light had come on in her head. "You're right!" she exclaimed. "That's exactly what's been going on."

As we discussed the situation, she developed an action plan for her current project. She began using and circumventing the *20's*. Martha identified a few key *21's* who were not afraid to help her. She was able to sell most of her ideas and opened the first truly modern office that the company had ever staffed. In a matter of a few months, over the objections of some of the *20's*, Martha was offered a promotion by one of the *21's*.

The reasons she was given for not accepting her ideas varied from the general, such as "We've never done it that way before," to the specific, such as "We just can't afford that right now." The reasons that the *21's* gave for offering her a promotion were, "We need some new ideas" and "We need someone who can find the funding." *20's* see opportunities.

A short time later she came by my office to say good-bye. She had declined the promotion. She and her husband had decided to start their own business, a property management and procurement consulting service. Theirs would be a company made up *entirely* of *21's*: the two of them. And they are doing quite well. Martha's story points out a corollary of the Theory of *21*: smaller companies have a smaller ratio of *20's* than do larger companies. In fact, for every layer of management there is a proportionate increase in the percentage of *20's*.

> **Smaller organizations tend to have fewer 20's**

This is easily explained by two facts of corporate life: (1) As any company grows, the chief executive officer loses some of his or her control over the people who staff it and, (2) *20's* have to eat, too.

I was doing some sales training for a large company that made orthopedic implants, you know, hips, knees, etc. I became friends with the Senior Vice President of sales who employee number was five. He was a *21* with a long, successful track record. Now that the company had more than 400 employees, he was dismayed to find that some *20's* had crept in and were saying things to customers like, "We have never done it that way before," "we have rules and policies," and other such negative statements.

We were talking one day and he said, "You know what I don't like about our growth? Our salespeople come in to the home office and stick their head in the door and ask me to go out for a beer and I cannot go. There is just too much work and too many people."

Chapter Four: The Positive Twenty (+20)

What he was saying was that as organizations grow leaders lose direct influence with the workers. There are to many demands and too little time. This creates an open door for the *20's*.

Consider the fact that the top dog in any company loses some control as the business grows. Take any company or corporation, large or small, and examine its origin. You'll find one common thread in the history of most corporations, large or small. Most companies begin small or as a one-person operation. Even a major corporation, with a million employees, once had a sole proprietor. Henry Ford initially worked alone in his shop. General Motors was formed by the merger of several automobile manufacturers, each having been formed by a individual, such as Ransom Olds, who built the Oldsmobiles. It was Mr. Singer who originally built the sewing machines, and Woolworth's still bears the name of its first proprietor.

When the new company started out, its founder was able to be very selective in hiring new employees. Since most entrepreneurs are *21's*, most of the people hired were also *21's*. As time went on, the founder began delegating as many of the routine duties as he or she could, and one of the first to be passed out was the chore of hiring and firing. At some point, a *+20* found their way onto the payroll. *+20's* are the pioneers for all the *20's* since they can pass for *21's*. The busy *21* founder of the company inadvertently brings in a *+20* and the decline has begun.

Once the *+20's* are established in a company, the erosion has started. The second fact of corporate life now comes into play: *20's* have to eat, too. *20's* are living breathing human beings and require all the necessities of life that a *21* does. The

Once the +20's are inside an organization, the erosion has started

problem for the *20's* is that they cannot tolerate an environment in which they must change or grow. They need an environment in which they can get by without either of these pressures. So once a *+20* has gained entry into an organization, more *20's* follow. The *20's* recruit other *20's* with comments like: "We need more people like you in our company." *20's* understand what this means. Their hidden motivation is to produce an environment that is compatible with the *+20* work style. Both *20's*, the one hiring and the one being hired, are served well with this arrangement. One gains the opportunity to earn a living and the other adds a *20* to help support all of the other *20's*.

As the company continues to grow, the original *21's* and the subsequent *21's* rise to the executive offices. Even though the company is being eroded at the bottom by *20's*, the *21's* still maintain some level of control.

There comes the day for each entrepreneur when the business is no longer fun. This usually occurs when the *20's* have thoroughly penetrated the organization. At this point the wise *21* will either clean house or sell out.

When I started my own business, I decided that we would keep the business small enough to filter out the *20's* before they got a toehold in the company. The business must be fun, and as long as I enjoy it, we will continue. If it stops being fun we will all go do something else.

Smaller organizations tend to have fewer *20's* because the *20's* are weeded out in the employment process. Larger companies have more than their share of *20's* because there is less control in the hiring process and because once the *20's* have penetrated an organization they tend to multiply.

Here is a graphic representation of this aspect of the Theory of *21*. In any organization there is a management pyramid that can be used to identify the management structure. At the top of the pyramid is

Chapter Four: The Positive Twenty (+20)

the top executive. Below the top is a layer of management that reports directly to the top. Each subsequent layer will have more individuals until the final layer is reached. This layer represents the entry-level employees.

When the entrepreneur *21* begins his business, he surrounds himself with other *21's*. His company is staffed at all levels with *21's* and is represented like this:

21
21 21 21
21 21 21 21 21

As the company grows and the original *21* begins delegating more responsibility, the infiltration begins. At some point a *+20* (represented as *+20* in the chart), because of his resemblance to a *21*, makes his way onto the payroll:

21
21 21 21
21 21 +20 21 21

This *+20* is the pioneer for the *20's*. Once entrenched in an organization, the *+20* will recruit other *20's*, both *+20's* and *-20's*. Then the *+20* will use his masquerade and/or his longevity with the company to move into middle management. Soon the management pyramid looks like this:

21
21 +20 21
21 +20 21 -20 21

As time goes by, the organization grows and the *20's* proliferate. The remaining *21's* rise to the top, but because there are more

91

people in the organization, there are more and more *20's*. The percentage of *20's* increases until the *21's* are grossly outnumbered. The *20's* permeate the organization at all levels and finally stop the business from being fun for the entrepreneur. This is what the organization looks like when the time comes for the original *21* to bow out:

21
 -20 21 +20 +20 -20
-20 +20 -20 +20 -20 +20 -20

Take a look at the organization in which you work or sell and analyze the management pyramid. Look at your circle of friends, the organization of your civic group or any other universe of people. This will give you an idea of where your ideas need to be for them to succeed. There is no organization in which an idea cannot be sold. I know that, because I have sold in all types of pyramids. There is no organization that cannot be brought up to a level of performance that will please a *21*. The organization in which innovative ideas are most easily solved has this structure:

21
21 21 21
21 21 21 21 21

And the toughest structure in which to succeed as a *21* is:

+20
-20 +20 -20
-20 +20 -20 +20 -20

Chapter Four: The Positive Twenty (+20)

I won a trip to Acapulco for my sales results one year. The customer organization that I sold to was just like the one above. So it *can be* done. It took a lot of time wading past the *20's* and forcing them into a position where they acknowledged they needed my product and me. It was time and energy consuming. Frankly, except for the trip to Acapulco and the self-satisfaction, it almost wasn't worth it, because the resources spent on the sales will never be recovered through their profits.

One of the strongest characteristics of the *+20's* is their inability to make decisions. *-20's* always make a quick decision, and the answer is always no. *21's* make decisions readily, maybe not instantly, and their response to good ideas is always positive. But *+20's* just don't make any decisions at all. *+20's* don't realize that not making a decision *is* making a decision: it is making the decision not to decide.

> **-20"s make quick and negative decisions; +20's make slow negative decisions**

That may sound like a lot of double talk, but there is an important principle there. Once an issue arises, it must be resolved one way or the other. A decision is made either to act or not to act. If action is selected, the action is either positive or negative. This scenario is carried out *every* time an issue arises. Some people think that they can ignore the issue and it will either go away or else resolve itself. These people are *+20's*.

Any circumstance that requires action starts this process. In it simplest form, there is the cafeteria line. The *-20's* order "the usual," the *21's* order whatever they want, and the *+20's* try to find a way not to make a decision. Cafeteria lines demand a lot of decision making. Besides choosing an entree, you must also choose an appetizer, vegetables, a drink, maybe dessert, and so forth. The *+20* will typically have the same as the person ahead ordered or choose the daily special where everything is predetermined.

Another common example is the company memorandum. Every day millions of literary masterpieces called company memorandums are created and usually distributed via email. People categorize themselves by the way they react to these memorandums.

The *-20's* read the document and respond by explaining why any action proposed can't, shouldn't or won't be done. The *21's* will read the memorandum and determine how the information can be used to further their cause. The *+20's* won't read it at first, but will make a mental note to handle it - tomorrow. When the *+20's* finally get around to reading it, any action that is required by the memo will not be attempted until absolutely necessary. *+20's* do not realize that not doing anything with an action item, such as a memo, is making a decision not to do something.

When a *21* approaches a *20* with an idea, the *20* is forced to respond. We have seen that the *-20* will begin his "It can't/shouldn't/won't be done" monologue. The *+20* has to make a decision: to act or not to act. The *+20* will usually choose not to act but to give positive reinforcement that will, it is hoped, detain the *21* long enough for the momentum to die.

This is a common ploy by *+20's* because it has been successful. *21's* are often deceived by *+20's* long enough for the enthusiasm that they have generated to begin to wane. The one thing that a *21* must do is to keep the issue hot. The most important thing for a *+20* is to cool the issue down.

Once a *+20* has managed to slow the project, can anything be done to reverse the damage?

Chapter Four: The Positive Twenty (+20)

There are a number of approaches that the astute *21* can take when he or she realizes that a *+20* has managed to interfere with the project. The first priority, obviously, is to neutralize the *+20*.

The real world sometimes comes as a shock to me and Shirley Temple. I believe that everyone is salvageable; if I can succeed, everybody can. Don't fool yourself into thinking that you can convert this *+20* into a *21*; remember, born-again *21's* are rare. If

> THE MOST IMPORTANT INGREDIENTS FOR NEUTRALIZING THE *+20* ARE HONESTY AND SINCERITY.

you attempt to confront and eliminate the entrenched *+20*, you will probably only succeed in creating antagonism and strong opposition. That may be the end result anyway, but you can save yourself a lot of grief by setting your feelings aside, concentrating on your goal, and making an attempt to neutralize the *+20*.

Neutralizing the *+20* usually begins with the expression of gratitude for all the assistance the *+20* has provided. You should be able to do that sincerely because this person has taught you a valuable lesson: a lesson in perseverance of a lesson in Twentyism. Then explain to the *+20* that you want to pursue your idea and that you would like for him or her to assist you. You know that in all likelihood they will decline, since participation would require them to risk failure, which *20's* are not willing to do. Nevertheless, your gesture gives the *+20* the feeling that you respect them enough to ask for their assistance. Since respect is usually reciprocated, the *+20* will show respect for you by not openly or actively opposing you. This will usually keep them from slowing the momentum you generate in the future.

- ***Thank them***
- ***Ask for their help***
- ***Agree to take the risk/blame***

If this process, or some similar effort, does not neutralize the *+20*, move ahead anyway. You have already spent enough of your energy on this person. Understand the *+20's* position so that you can manage the results of his opposition. Put their name on your list of *20's*, make a note of why they said your idea would not fly, and adjust your tactical plan as necessary.

If you are an experienced salesperson, you may recognize this particular *+20* as the "gatekeeper," to use a marketing term for the person who specializes in keeping outsiders out. Selling around the gatekeeper is an art that has puzzled more than a few salespeople. I am about to share with you my tried-and-true method of working around the *+20* gatekeeper.

First of all, you never go around a gatekeeper, you go above them. What is the difference? If you go around them, they will catch you on the way back down and they will hurt you every chance and every way they can. When you go above them, you go with them or with their blessing. Now why would a *20* of any sort take you to their boss or allow you to go up the ladder with their blessing? There is always a reason and it varies with every *+20*. What works with one may or may not work with another.

You should understand by now that your strategy should be to neutralize the *+20*. You don't want them to work against you, and you don't necessarily want any more of their "help." The secret is to put the *+20* in a position where he can't lose. Convince the *+20* that you will proceed with your plan, and that if it fails, you will be solely responsible. Also convince the *+20* that if you are successful, they will share in the glory.

To accomplish this we must first answer the question, *"Why is it in this person's best interest to do what I want them to do?"* Once we have answered this question, we know how to cause the antics of the

Chapter Four: The Positive Twenty (+20)

+20 to work for us. Until we can answer this question, we spend our time with the +20 seeking the answer, not trying to convince them. Everybody has a reason why they will do something as long as it is moral and legal.

Sound impossible? It isn't. It isn't easy, by any means - if it were easy, everyone could do it, not just *21's*. Find out what the +20 really wants. Do they want recognition? Offer them that. Do they want peace and quiet? Offer them that. Find out what they want and show them how your achieving your goal will help them achieve their goal.

> **Find out what the +20 really wants.**

The first step is to go back to your *21* Worksheet. Make sure that your goal is clearly in focus. Lay out a plan with strategies and tactics to accomplish your goal. Identify the true decision maker and map out how you will approach him or her. Determine that the credit for every successful move will be shared with the +20, whether he deserves it or not. Most *+20's* have talked enough about doing positive things that they feel they deserve the credit for anything positive that happens around them.

There is a twofold purpose in allowing the +20 to share in the success that they originally opposed. First if your efforts are successful and you haven't included them, they may quickly turn into a *-20* and begin actively opposing you. Second, no matter how your project turns out, this person will still be the gatekeeper. The next time you confront them they will remember what happened and will respond accordingly.

I was assigned to an account whose gatekeeper, I was told, was a +20 with a chip on his shoulder. My predecessor had circumvented

97

this person and had succeeded in making a large sale. He also succeeded in alienating the gatekeeper.

In retaliation for our previous success, the gatekeeper rejected virtually every proposal from my company. He started to make buying decisions more rapidly than before, and the decision always went in favor of our competitor. On a number of occasions he did not even allow us to bid on projects.

As soon as I was assigned to the account, I made a list of strategies and tactics I would use to accomplish the impossible goal of selling our product to this company for use in their headquarters location. I knew that once this was accomplished, it would be easier to sell our products and services in other locations throughout the country. The first strategy was to neutralize the gatekeeper, and I made a tactical plan to accomplish that.

The second strategy was to place my proposal in front of the executive vice-president, who I had identified as the true decision maker. I had a list of tactics to accomplish that as well, but concentrated on the first strategy.

> **The Theory of 21 requires mental exercises**

Application of the Theory of 21 requires mental exercises. It is very important to think through what you intend to do before you act. This does not call for tremendous intelligence, all it requires is that you take a realistic look at where you are and where you want to be and then decide how you can get there. Don't think in terms of how you, with your unique set of talents and skills, can attain your goal. What works for others may not work for you, and what works for you probably won't work for someone else.

Chapter Four: The Positive Twenty (+20)

Shortly after I was assigned to the account, I called this gentleman and made an appointment for lunch. This was to be our first meeting, and I knew he would want to unload on me about how miserable our company was. If I allowed him to do that in his office, he would have a major advantage and I would have made neutralizing this person an even more difficult task.

The restaurant I selected served the *+20's* favorite dessert. All through the appetizer and entree he told me, in great detail, how my company had mishandled the account. I allowed him to vent his feelings until I thought he was ready to consider a new approach to managing our relationship. I sincerely apologized for the way he felt he had been treated, and assured him that he would see a new side to our company.

I honored my pledge to work with the *+20* because I believe that honesty and sincerity are the two most important weapons in combating the *20's*.

After a week or two had passed, the *+20* asked me to accompany him on a business trip to Washington, D.C. He said he wanted me to assist him in auditing one of his distant offices. I supposed that this was to be a test of my sincerity since my employer would expect me to make recommendations to upgrade our equipment in that location. The *+20* would say that he intended to downgrade, that is, to remove much of the equipment there. Then he would watch my reaction.

We made our initial study, and it was obvious that the Washington office sorely needed a new, upgraded system. The *+20* said that he thought a downgrade was the answer. I had reviewed my *21* Worksheet and realized that I had not neutralized this *+20*. I was therefore not yet in a position to contradict him. I bought some time by telling him that I wanted to take my findings back to Atlanta for computer analysis, which was standard procedure.

The day of our trip, over breakfast, I managed to break some of the ice and have the *+20* talk more about himself. In the course of the conversation, he revealed that he was an avid member of the Optimist Club. He went on to say that he was in charge of the programming for the following month. I explained that I was an after-dinner speaker and offered my services. He was excited to find a fresh voice and a new topic, so we set a date and chose the topic of "Call Me," a motivational talk on communication.

Between the time that we returned from our trip and the time that I addressed the Optimist Club, I polished my proposal for the headquarters location and put together a formal recommendation for the Washington office. The *+20* was not sufficiently neutralized for a major sale, but I did manage to close a few smaller sales that had been lingering around for some time. That reassured me that I was on the right track, and it reassured my boss that I was really out selling. The small sales were nice, but I wanted the BIG ones! Now, here is how you use *your unique talents and abilities* to move through the *+20's*. My talent is public speaking and I used it to the fullest the day I spoke to the Optimist Club. I gave it everything I had.

There was a standing ovation following my talk - a rare occurrence, I learned later. The *+20* became the hero of the hour and was warmly congratulated by the entire membership for finding such a fine speaker.

The next day I was in the office of the *+20* with my headquarters proposal. The time was right. I expected him to decline, and he did. I explained that he could be the hero on this one - all I wanted was the sale. He had declined, but he moved out of the way. His reason: "they would never buy it".

> **Use your unique talents and skills to manage the 20's**

Chapter Four: The Positive Twenty (+20)

I sold the headquarters project and, as a result of that and other successes, was promoted before closing the Washington deal. My successor on the account was Ed, one of my favorite *21's*. Ed was aware of what I had accomplished and knew a lot about how I had managed to succeed with this *+20*. Ed and I talked and mapped out a strategy for him to follow to close the Washington proposal.

Ed acknowledged that he was not a public speaker and would have to use his own talents to be successful on this account. We assessed Ed's abilities and decided which of his strengths would work best for him in this situation. He then defined his strategies and tactics and attacked the account.

Ed's strongest talent is his ability to get along with almost anyone and his uncanny ability to accomplish the seemingly impossible tasks inside his company - tasks such as finding out-of-stock equipment, cutting shipping and installation times, and gaining "impossible" concessions for his customers.

I introduced Ed to the *+20* gatekeeper, and immediately Ed asked if there was anything he could do for the customer. Just as we had anticipated, the customer asked for a favor. He wanted an obsolete, unavailable device for one of his distant offices. He had asked for this device before but had been turned down by the *-20's* in our company. Ed showed his sincerity by procuring the item and having it delivered to the office where it was needed.

From then on, whenever anyone in the customer's organization needed anything from our company, they would simply tell the *+20*, who would pass the request on to Ed. Ed was making the *+20* a hero inside his own organization, just as I had done, but he was doing it his own way, with his own skills.

After a few successes, Ed figured he was ready to ask the *+20* for the order on the Washington project, the deal I hadn't been able to close. After a few false starts involving the expected, menial rewrites of the proposal, Ed became convinced that the *+20* was stalling, waiting for the momentum to dissipate. Ed pushed for the close and received the expected reply: "they wouldn't approve it". Ed explained that he would again make him a hero, but the *+20* wouldn't accept his promise because there was too much risk. However, he did move aside, neutralized by Ed's hard work, and Ed sold the Washington project to the senior vice president, the one who would "never approve it".

Ed's story points out how he used his talents to successfully move around the *+20*. Maybe you don't think that the ability to work with people or having the determination to work hard are talents. And maybe you don't think you have any special talents. Think again. Most people enjoy the things they do well, and the things you do well are your talents. Therefore: whatever you enjoy doing most is your talent. Because you enjoy it, you don't think of it as a skill, but it is.

Applying the Theory of 21 allows you to use your talents and skills to move around and through the *+20's* to accomplish your impossible goals. As Frank Sinatra sang, you do it your way.

At best, *+20's* have plans to *become* successes; they have no plans to *be* successes. Let's look at the difference.

If a *+20* sets out to do anything positive, it is usually with the implicit understanding that, in the long run, it will never work out. Therefore, they will give some merit to trying to accomplish something. They will give limited credibility to the concept that it might actually work out. Therefore, the *+20's* give enough lip service and halfhearted effort to a few ideas so that one or two

Chapter Four: The Positive Twenty (+20)

actually happen. Lacking any real desire for long-term success, their achievements are short lived.

The *+20's* are everywhere. They are the public officials who don't deliver on their promises. They are the service people who promise repairs that are not made or are not made in the agreed-upon time. The *+20's* are the members of your church or civic organization who accepted positions of leadership supposedly to make things happen but have accomplished nothing. *+20's* are the people in your organization who have begun numerous projects and completed few. The person who attends committee meetings week after week, promising that the report will be ready next week, is a *+20*. "Next week" is another way of saying "tomorrow." *+20's* have enough initiative to promise to begin a project, but not enough to see it through.

To salespeople, the most aggravating of them all is the *+20* gatekeeper. For everyone, the most exasperating is the repairman who never completes his task. No matter how long he keeps your item or how often he attempts to correct the problem, it never works right. I have used the Theory of 21 to master these *+20's*, too. I rarely have trouble with service people any longer.

Several years ago I bought a new car. Like many new automobiles, it had a few problems that needed correcting. I left it with the dealer for a day and picked it up, only to find that the trouble was still there. I took the car back and had a heart-to-heart talk with the rookie mechanic who had been assigned to my car. He vowed to fix it but being a *+20*, he promised more than he performed, and the car was no better off. Since sincerity is an essential element in managing the *+20's*, how could I honestly manage this one? What could I *sincerely* say to him to neutralize him?

When I came to pick up my car and found that it still wasn't repaired, I sought out the young mechanic. I told him how impressed

I was with anyone who could begin to understand the complex inner workings of that car and explained that I thought there was a manufacturing defect in the car since he could not fix it. He knew that wasn't so, and so did I. But it got him off the hook and out of my way. As I approached the service manager to explain about the "manufacturing defect," the mechanic began looking more closely at my car. Suddenly he found the source of the problem, fixed it, and saved the service manager a lot of grief from me. My praise for his work convinced the mechanic that he was a hero.

From then on, whenever my car was taken in for service, the same mechanic always took care of it personally. Instead of doing the least he could do, he usually went the extra mile. When the bumper needed work, he repaired it and also tightened the fan belt and adjusted some other things--all at no charge. Was the *+20* mechanic evolving into a *21*?

On rare occasions, *+20's* do evolve into *21's*. The metamorphosis changes one human being from a difficult obstacle into a potent innovator. Success and failure are reserved for the *21's*, so when a Positive *20* assumes the responsibility of trying to become a *21*, at that moment he *is* a *21*.

You are about to learn more about the *21's* and about how to mold a *21* out of a *+20*.

The most exiting part of the Theory of 21 is the *21's*. We have spent enough time on the *20's*; now for the best part . . .

Chapter Five

The 21's

An old man was sitting at the gate to the city when a stranger approached.

"Tell me, old man," said the stranger, "have you lived here long?"

"All my Life," was the reply.

"Well, tell me this: how will I find the people here?" asked the stranger.

The old man thought for a moment and asked, "How were they where you came from?"

"Terrible," the stranger responded. "They were the biggest bunch of thieves and cutthroats I've ever seen. They would steal the shirt right off your back."

"You'll find them the same way here," the old man said.

Some time later, another stranger approached the city, saw the old man, and asked the same question: "How will I find the people here?"

The old man thought for a moment and asked, "How were they where you came from?"

"Oh," said the stranger, "they were the finest bunch of people you would ever want to meet. They'd give you the shirt off their back."

"You'll find them the same way here," said the old man.

It is true that we find what we are looking for. *21*'s find success, and they find it everywhere they go. As you will discover in this chapter, there are reasons why the *21* finds success in the same areas where the *20* finds failure. *20's* and *21*'s all live in the same world, meet the same people, and see the same events. The *21*'s come away from these experiences with accomplishments while the *20's* come away with nothing new.

Two men, Mr. A and Mr. B, enter a restaurant and both order lobster. The waitress brings a platter with two lobsters on it. One lobster is large and juicy, the other small and dried-up. Mr. A reaches over and takes the nicer lobster, puts it on his plate, and begins breaking off the claws. Mr. B says, "Well, I guess that's the rudest thing I've ever seen. "Mr. A replies, "Why? What would you have done?" Mr. B says, "I'd have taken the smaller one." "You've got it!" Mr. A responds.

To understand the Theory of 21, you must first understand the difference between "natural" and "average." The average American is 8.5 pounds overweight. That is not natural. The average American smokes 1.4 cigarettes a day - average but not natural. Sneezing and coughing are natural; filling one's lungs with a carcinogenic tar isn't.

The average person will do things that are not natural. Too many average people believe that things that have not been done cannot, should not, or will not

Average people do things that are not natural

Chapter Five: The 21's

be done. But that is not natural. Change, and the occurrence of new events, is natural.

If you study the behavior of children, you will see that children believe that almost anything is possible. Adults call it "make-believe" when a child pretends to be a doctor or a scientist. But in fact, for that moment in time, the child is a doctor. If left alone, I believe that the child would eventually become a doctor. Of course it would take an extensive education and so forth, but until a child is told that he is not a doctor, he will continue to believe that he can be one.

The child is "told" that he is not a doctor in a variety of ways. If his brother or sister becomes ill, the parents either nurse that sibling back to health without any assistance from the child, or they call for the help of an actual doctor. Either way, the child gets the message that he is not doing the doctoring. Even if he offers to help, the parents are likely to shoo him away.

But take the case of Jimmy. At the age of four, Jimmy announced that he wanted to become an aeronautical engineer. His parents didn't understand why or how he knew he wanted to be an aeronautical engineer, but they never attempted to discourage him. By the time Jimmy finished third grade, he also knew that he wanted to work for Lockheed. After achieving honors at Georgia Tech, Jimmy spent a year flying a helicopter in Vietnam and distinguished himself in that role. There were numerous job offers for Jimmy because of his education and experience, some of them quite lucrative, Jimmy turned them all down and waited for an offer from Lockheed. He is still at Lockheed today.

In 1867, American Secretary of State W.H. Seward struck a deal with Russia to purchase the territory of Alaska for just over seven million dollars. Many people, the **20's**, *saw* *nothing but folly. The deal eventually became known as "Seward's Icebox".*

Where others saw folly, Seward saw opportunity.

*The newly acquired frozen area known as the Alaska Territory also represented opportunity to Alec McDonald. While the **20's** were content to sit and ridicule the seven million dollar real estate purchase, McDonald went to Alaska. After all, **21's** seek first hand experience, **20's** dwell on second hand information, sometimes known as gossip.*

What Alec McDonald found was gold. He eventually mined twenty million dollars worth of gold for himself. In other words, his personal wealth from this venture was nearly three times what the U.S. had paid for the property. At today's tax rates, McDonald's taxes would have paid for the entire purchase.

Today, the *20's* will say, "Yes. That was then and this is now. That could never happen again." The *21*'s are the people who continue to seek new opportunities. After all, it wasn't that long ago that another gold, Black Gold, was discovered around Alec McDonald's digs. The estimates of the value of the oil reserves in Alaska now reach into the billions of dollars.

You and everyone else were born *21*'s. *20's* are the products of our society, a society that endorses and encourages the unnatural attitudes, one of which is to oppose change regardless of its potential to improve our lives.

Somewhere in our past, we were taught the attitudes of the *20's* and that mind-set was reaffirmed by too many of the people we knew, including our friends, our schoolteachers, and our ministers. This is

Chapter Five: The 21's

normal, though not natural. And it should not be surprising, since most people are *20's* and people teach what they believe. Too many people lose the innocence of their youth, become *20's*, and then become the makers and molders of more *20's*. They begin to expect to find Twentyism everywhere we go, and we are usually not disappointed. This is the average, normal scheme of things. But it is not natural.

You can usually tell what a person expected from any given situation by what they found. I have seen people leaving a motivational seminar with a bounce in their step and determination in their eyes, while others, the *20's*, left grumbling about the "phony hype." The first expected motivation and the others expected phony hype.

> **You can usually tell what a person expected from any given situation by what they found.**

20's do not expect new ideas to sell, and their ideas don't sell. *21's* expect their ideas to sell, and they do. People who expect to be passed over for promotion usually are. Others think that they do not have a chance of winning a contest or a game, and they lose. *21's* believe that they will win even when all others may be telling them that they do not have a chance, and they emerge winners.

I have seen this phenomenon occur in the greatest and smallest events of life. During the busiest shopping season, people tell me that they have to park a great distance from the malls and shops, and they do. I usually park by the door. Some people expect illness and look sick; others expect health and look well. Two employees join the company at the same time, one expecting success and one mediocrity. The first retires from the top floor, the other retires from a lower floor.

As you may have surmised, this is all to point out a basic fact: Being a *21* is a mind-set. You must believe that the impossible is possible. You must understand that the difficult can be accomplished.

> **Being a 21 is a mindset**

Here's an example. Could you sell horse fodder for human consumption?

In the late 1800's, a Dutchman named Ferdinand Schumacher attempted to do just that. He had devised a meat substitute made from oats. He was already in the business of feeding farm animals, so this was a natural extension of his existing business. The idea of expanding into the business of selling to humans was very exciting and promising - or so he thought.

Schumacher suggested that his oat concoction be substituted for breakfast at a time when that meal lasted usually sixty minutes and included several meats, breads and a side order of sweets. His suggestion was ridiculed in papers all over the country. However, his product, Quaker Oats, became an American legend.

It gets better. To make his success happen, Schumacher chose to use some untried ideas. He advertised nationally at a time when banks refused to loan money to companies who advertised. The banks believed that only snake oil salesmen advertised.

Schumacher also pioneered the concept of point of sale advertising. Grocery stores were not the self-service supermarkets they are today. In fact, the goods were all behind a counter and the proprietor would retrieve whatever item the customer wanted. From a distance, like the distance

Chapter Five: The 21's

from the customer to the shelf, all products looked pretty much alike. Schumacher did the unthinkable: he used different colors on his packages. Instead of the usual black ink on brown paper, Quaker Oats stood out with their red, white and blue packages.

As a result of what Ferdinand Schumacher did, the cereal industry was born. And today, the cereals are packaged in brightly colored boxes.

So what distinguishes the Theory of 21 from any other teaching that espouses the virtues of having the right attitude?

None of this is new to those of you who are students of positive thinking. Numerous books have been written and thousands of seminars have been conducted to teach the power of positive thought. But the problem with some positive thinkers is that they are unable to translate their positive ideas into results. The positive attitude is there, but the accomplishments are missing. This is where the Theory of 21 can be of invaluable assistance.

Remember, the basic difference between *20's* and *21*'s is accomplishment. There are many people running around with positive attitudes who want to succeed, but who have not begun to

> **Remember, the basic difference between *20's* and *21*'s is <u>accomplishment</u>.**

accomplish their goals. If you are one of these people, this chapter is for you.

For the Law to work, you must first have positive attitude. It is unlikely that you would even attempt to become a *21* in the first place without a strong, positive attitude. I mention it here to remind you of the importance of having the correct mindset.

But positive thinking alone is not enough. There must be action if anything is to be accomplished. Generally speaking, greater action produces greater results. To maximize the results, maximize the actions. To maximize the actions, have a plan. It is really that simple:

Positive Thinking + Positive Action = Positive Results.

The more you add to the left side of the equation, the more you add to the right side. Remove either element from the left side of the equations and the whole thing falls apart. All of the positive thinking in the world is useless when it is not accompanied with positive action. All of the positive action in the world yields nothing when the thought behind it are not positive.

That sounds so simple but I see daily manifestations of people misusing this seemingly simple formula. There are thousands of people who have their dreams and who are waiting for them to manifest themselves. They have their daily affirmations, they have pictures of their dreams so they can do their imaging or visualization and yet nothing is happening for them. Nothing will ever happen for them. Things don't happen for us, they happen because of us - specifically because of our actions. All of the thinking, visualization and other mental exercises will produce nothing. Prayer will not make your dreams happen. Didn't the Apostle Paul say that, "Faith without works is dead"?

Harrison Ford rocketed to fame by playing the role of Hans Solo in the Star Wars trilogy. He will tell you that while others were saying, "May the force be with you", he was saying, "Force yourself!"

But positive action alone is not enough either. Doing all of the right things with a negative attitude will not bring the results we want. Suppose someone suggested that I call Mr. Adams to see if he would

Chapter Five: The 21's

help me attain my goals. My response is, "He won't help me. I'll call him, but there's no way he is going to help me do what I want to do". How do you think the call on Mr. Adams is going to go? I'll probably open the call with, "You don't want to help me, do you?", or some similar self defeating approach.

The Theory of 21 incorporates a proven method to maximize the results, the successes, the accomplishments you will achieve. For the *21* who knows how to use other *21*'s and knows how to move around the *20's*, nothing is impossible.

NOTHING IS IMPOSSIBLE. You can accomplish your goal whatever it is, by applying the principles of the Law.

The first step in being a *21* is to know what you want. Have clearly defined goals. If goals are not written, quantified and dated, they are probably not very specific and your mind cannot focus on making your success happen.

The second step is to have a plan, but without a goal there can be no plan. Know what you want!

In my seminars and in one-on-one situations, I ask this question: **"What do you want to accomplish with your life?"** To me, that is the most important issue: what is your purpose in life, what is your vision for yourself? I do not understand why anyone would choose to live one day at a time with no thought for tomorrow and no goals.

Fortunately, I see very few people who give no thought to goals at all. What I do see is a lot of people who do not exactly know what they want, or who know what they want but aren't sure how to go about attaining it. Is that where you are?

Right now, not two minutes from now but right now, think of what you would do with the rest of your life if you could do anything. I want you to "blue sky" on this one for a moment. Then I want you to formulate a one-sentence answer. We will expound on it later.

Formulate your answer. Repeat your answer several times in your mind so that it will be implanted there. Each word is critical. Now let's discuss your initial response to one of the most important questions that you will ever address. Did your response begin with something like: "Someday I would like to . . . ?" If it did, we have identified the first obstacle to your attaining your impossible goal. Pull out every calendar you can find and see which one has a "someday" on it. It doesn't exist and it will never come. Waiting on "someday" is the single biggest obstacle to becoming a *21*. It has tripped up more potential *21*'s than any other single obstacle, and has become a dead end for quite a few *20's*. Put a date on your goal.

Imagine what you would do with the rest of your life if you could do anything at all.

There is a normal tendency to act when the time is "right." I am convinced that the "right" time comes along so infrequently that it is not worth the pursuit for anyone. If you are waiting for the "right" time, the "someday," then plan to stay right where you are from now on.

Wally Amos decided to bake cookies for a living. He knew that was what he wanted to do, and he was convinced that he would enjoy doing it and that he would succeed. His *20's* explained why he couldn't, shouldn't, wouldn't succeed at this business. The major bakeries had the market sewn up. Wally was undercapitalized; he did not have the credentials to run the business or to raise the money he needed. And besides, the price of sugar was at an all-time high - the time was not right to start a cookie business.

Chapter Five: The 21's

One of Wally Amos's other goals was to live in Hawaii. After Famous Amos cookies took off, Wally opened another plant in Hawaii and moved there. His cookies are now sold nationwide, are considered a delicacy by some, and command a premium price. When Wally travels to the mainland, he brings along his favorite toy, a custom vehicle. Wally Amos does everything with class, and there is no "wrong" time for a class act. Incidentally, thirty minutes with Amos will make a *21* out of almost any Positive *20*. When someone offered to buy his company for a price most of us would consider to be a fortune, Wally sold out. Why? Because he has already set his next set of goals and was ready to move ahead.

If Wally Amos had waited for the price of sugar to drop, the cost of labor would probably have gone up, and many other components of his overhead, such as rent, flour, and packaging costs, might have increased in cost. So the time would not have been "right" then, either. But more important than that, while Wally was waiting for the "right" time he would not have been selling cookies. He would not have been building a business and he would not have made the money from his cookies. What he would have been doing is working at something that was not what he really wanted instead of something he really enjoyed,

Think about this, when Wally first imagined himself having his own cookie company, a portion of his market went away every day he delayed. Every day people ate cookies and the cookies they ate weren't Wally's. The same is true for you. Every day that you delay making the commitment to begin your dream is a day *lost* to your dream. If your goal is to publish a book, then every day that you delay writing the book is a day that one of your potential readers buys another book. If your goal is to publish a magazine, then every month that you delay is an issue that will never be published. If your goal is to be the vice-president of your department, then every year you procrastinate and avoid making the decision to map out and follow a plan is one less year that you will be a VP.

So, set a date.

Set a realistic date but don't put it too far off. You will learn that once you have a targeted goal, things may begin happening faster than you may have thought possible. People more often set their targeted date too far off than too soon, so be realistic but plan on stretching yourself.

> **Set a realistic date but not too far out...**

Whenever I am being interviewed, I like to turn the interview around and find out what type of person the interviewer is and what their agenda is. After all, if they are a *20*, I need to know that. So when the interviewer began asking me about the first edition of The Theory of 21, I began asking questions of the interviewer.

Her name was Diane. I asked her what she would do if she could do anything she wanted. Diane is a reporter for a business newspaper, and her goal is to have her own magazine, one along the lines of *The New Yorker*. I asked her to formulate her goal, and she began with the dreaded "someday." I made a suggestion: "Do you have any friends in the paste-up department at your paper? Ask one of them to make a mockup of your first magazine cover. You decide the typeset and the cover story. Then take the cover home and hang it in a prominent place where you will see it every day."

Once Diane does this, she will begin adding the headlines for the cover and this will cause her to think of the people she will need to write the stories behind the headlines. Events will occur and have a significant impact on her: she will begin thinking of them in terms of potential articles for her magazine. These events should assist her in establishing a target for the first issue. She will meet people who

Chapter Five: The 21's

will strike her as potential employees, partners, or backers for her magazine. Once the date is established, her magazine will start to become a reality.

Visualization and imaging are important concepts. You need a point of focus, some visualization of your goal. If your goal is a new position in your company, write up a newspaper announcement or an internal memo of your promotion, and date it. Have a goal. If your goal is a job with another company, make yourself a new business card with the title you want on it, and date it. Have a goal.

> **You need a point of focus**

If your goal is to increase the membership of your organization from 25 to 250, then find a picture of 250 people and write the name of your organization on it and the date that you expect the group to attain that membership goal. Then hang the picture in a place that will often remind you of your goal and your targeted date.

What was your goal? Formulate it in your mind again. Does it sound something like: "Someday I want to . . ." or "Someday I wish to . . . "? If so, we may have identified the second obstacle to your achieving your impossible goal. Even if you replace the "someday" with a specific date, you still have a weakness. The Theory of 21 does not work for wants or wishes. As long as your goal is a want or a wish, it assumes little credence in your mind. We all have pipe dreams and daydreams, and for the most part they never happen. To have a goal that will survive the *20's*, you must *know* that your goal will happen. If you are not convinced, you will have little success convincing anyone else. So begin your goal with, "I will..."

Compare the goals above to this one: "Within the next six months I will have completed the manuscript of a full-length novel." Or to this one: "By this date next year I will have the title of Regional

Sales Manager." Do you see the difference? Can you feel the difference?

By restating your goals and putting them into positive, concrete terms, you will convince yourself and others that your goals are going to happen. What you sense on the outside is not as important as what is going on in your mind. We are learning that not only is the mind programmable, but it takes its programming from our deepest beliefs. If you recite something often enough, your inner self will begin believing it and your mind will program it to happen.

> **Goals function in the subconscious mind**

When you were a child, did you ever hear the story of *The Little Engine Who Could?* In this story, a small steam engine has to pull a long train up a hill, a seemingly impossible task. However, because she believes she can, and reinforces her belief by chanting "I think I can, I think I can" she succeeds.

In earlier chapters we discussed the *20's* and noted that they were easily discouraged by other *20's*. When a *20* has an idea, he does not usually take the time to convince himself that the idea *will* happen. His mind is not convinced. So when he hits the first obstacle, he is easily put off. In many cases, if you could get to the *20* at that point and tell him that his idea was a good one, he would try again. But then the next obstacle would become a dead end. He will not be able to persevere because he is not really convinced.

You know that you have the talent and the ability to accomplish your goal, don't you? You know that you understand what it takes to achieve what you want to achieve, and you know that you want it. So all you have to do is *do it*. If you are having doubts about your own abilities--we all do from time to time--try this: think about

> **Just do it**

Chapter Five: The 21's

individuals who are already doing what you want to do and compare yourself to them *objectively*. Are they superhuman? Is their intelligence at the genius level? I doubt it.

The only difference between you and the people who are doing what you would like to do is just that: they are doing it.

And the main reason that you aren't doing it is because you haven't tried.

Convince yourself, and the next step is to convince one other person. The other person you convince needs to be another **21**. Sharing your ideas with **20's** only leads to discouragement and frustration.

You are now ready to take on the **20's**, so as soon as you are convinced that you can accomplish your goal, go convince just one other person. If you are married, I recommend that the one person that you convince be your spouse. If you're not married, choose a friend who knows you well. You need to select a person who knows you well so that you cannot fool them in case you're really not convinced. The whole purpose of this effort is to solidify your conviction of your ability to accomplish your goal and to create synergy between you and someone else.

At this point you will have created momentum. As I said before, without commitment, this momentum can be stopped with the first obstacle. What you need now is a plan, a track to follow that will direct the momentum.

It's time for a **21** Worksheet. Fill in the blanks:

"I will accomplish the impossible goal of _____.
In order to do that, I must first accomplish the difficult tactics of:

1.
2.
3.
4.
5.
6.
7.
8.
9.
10.

The tasks I will use to do that are: (List your steps.)
1.
2.
3.
4.
5.

The Theory of 21 forces you to identify and examine the steps you need to take to accomplish your goal. Break them down into their simplest tasks. Don't leave anything out, because no matter how trivial a task may seem, it still must be done. These tasks are the benchmarks that will show you and others the progress you are making toward your goal. Most benchmarks should also be assigned a target date. As you identify each step, set a target date to complete that step, and then *do* it. These interim deadlines will motivate you one step at a time, and the composite of them will give you a more accurate feel for the date that your goal will be accomplished.

Chapter Five: The 21's

Up until now, you may never have begun the effort to be what you want to be. And for that reason, you have come no closer to attaining your goal. What you should be able to do now is take the first step.

If your goal is to achieve a higher position in your company - say, two levels above your current position - then the first strategy you need to detail is how to rise to the next level. What are the tasks that are necessary to accomplish that? Do you have any idea where to start? I have seen case after case where an idea never became reality because the person with the idea did not know where to start. This is a common malady that has tripped up a lot of people. There is an easy way to begin.

Instead of looking at the entire problem or opportunity all at once, try breaking it down into smaller components.

Two privates in the Army were assigned to a disciplinary work detail and told to move a two-ton pile of rocks, none of which were too heavy. One looked at the pile and said it was too large and much too heavy for two people to move. The other saw it and realized that no single rock was too large for a single person to move. Trying to decide on a plan of attack for achieving a new position in the corporation may not be as easy as moving a pile of rocks. If you simply cannot identify the first step, then the first step is obvious: identify the first step. You do that by asking people who should know, "How do I begin?"

This may be your first experience with a *20*, so you will need to keep track of your *20's* using this worksheet. In the future, you can make one of these lists on the back of your *21* Worksheet. Make a place to list the *20's* and their reasons for telling you that your goal cannot be accomplished. It should look something like this:

NAME	REASON
1. _____	_____
2. _____	_____
3. _____	_____
4. _____	_____
5. _____	_____
6. _____	_____
7. _____	_____
8. _____	_____
9. _____	_____
10. _____	_____
11. _____	_____
12. _____	_____
13. _____	_____
14. _____	_____
15. _____	_____
16. _____	_____
17. _____	_____
18. _____	_____
19. _____	_____
20. _____	_____

Whom are you going to ask? You are looking for advice on how to begin your quest toward your impossible goal, so what type of person are you to approach? First of all, find someone who has done what you want to do and someone who tried to accomplish your goal and failed. Both can give you enormous amounts of information. Using what you know already about *21*'s, try to find *21*'s, not *20's*. Those who have succeeded can tell you how they made their success happen for them. Their ideas may or MAY not work for you. The *21*'s who tried and did not succeed probably tried many different approaches and are probably thinking about yet

Chapter Five: The 21's

another way to make the success happen. This is the person who can actually teach you more than the one who succeeded. They can help prevent you from reinventing the wheel.

Ask these selected people how to start, and write down what they say. If they tell you that you cannot/should not/will not accomplish your goal, ask them why and put their name and reason on the back of your *21* Worksheet. If they say something like: "It won't be easy, but . . . " you have identified a valuable resource; take in all that they will tell you. They are being honest: if it were easy, everybody would be doing it. However, do not equate difficulty with unpleasantness. Even though your trip to your impossible goal may be difficult, it will also be enjoyable.

I have found that the person who says "Success came easily for me" either had a head start with some family money or else they enjoyed the work so much that he or she never saw the difficulties. Neither case will offer much help to you in trying to start off on the first step. Success is sometimes simple, but it is rarely easy.

In 1979 an immigrant named Joseph Nakash was competing with blue-blooded, well-heeled Gloria Vanderbilt for the designer jean dollars. Fifteen years earlier, Nakash was sleeping in bus and train stations because his $40-a-week job as a stock boy would not provide him any better housing. Mr. Nakash was able to save enough money to bring his brothers to this country, and the three of them built a company and created the Jordache fashion line. They each had to work long hours, but their hours and working conditions were an improvement on their previous life-styles. Their experience and common sense told them that the way to succeed was to advertise like crazy, and so they poured money into the now familiar Jordache ads. Gloria Vanderbilt and the Nakash brothers began the race from different *starting points, but reached the finish line together. They faced some similar hurdles and encountered their own unique hurdles. But all of these people enjoyed the race toward their goal.*

Why would people who are successful want to talk to you?

They probably do not have the time to spend talking to everyone who asks for their time. How are you to gain an audience with them? As a rule, they are very busy people. If they are ahead of you in the corporate structure, the rules may say that you cannot talk to them. If they are public figures, there will be rules that govern their time and their interfaces with other people.

Make yourself an exception to the rule.

This is the heart of the Theory of 21. This is also the most often misunderstood aspect of the Law, so I will take some time to explain it now. You are to make yourself an exception to the rule, but *you are never to break the rule*. There is an important difference. First of all, understand what rules are.

Rules are not laws, and there should be no exceptions to laws. For example, it is a law, not a rule, which requires us to stop at red lights. Trying to be an exception to that law could only be catastrophic. But rules are different. Rules are made to control the masses, and the masses are, you guessed it, *20's*. *20's* want and need rules because rules are the first step in blocking change. Rules are an easy out, and rules can be a valuable tool for controlling the *20's*. But if you look closely at most rules, you will see that they have control and limitation as their purpose. There are exceptions to this statement, of course, such as rules that require a certain amount of effort in order to be obeyed. Sales goals are rules that cause something to happen. But like most action-stimulating rules, sales objectives are governed by more rules.

For instance: the rule is that all salespeople must sell one million dollars' worth of goods every year or they will not be paid a bonus and will be subject to dismissal. That's the action-provoking rule. Behind this is a list of rules about where each salesperson can sell, what they must sell, what paper work must accompany each order, and so on. These are limiting rules.

If you break a rule, you ARE subjecting yourself to the possibility of all kinds of misery. But to be an exception to the rule means that you have permission from someone in authority to circumvent it. Why would anyone want to do that for you?

When I go into a place that has a sign that says "No Personal Checks Accepted," I write a check and the proprietor takes it. Why? Because he thinks my check is good and because he wants the business. And that in a nutshell is how you can be an exception to the rule.

There are two elements:

- You must appear worthy of the exception.
- There must be something in it for the person responsible for enforcing the rule.

The first element is something you earn. If you want to be a third-level manager and you are currently a first-level, the rules say that you must serve some time as a second-level. That is a rule for *20's*. Suppose a person clearly demonstrates that he can perform at the third level and that he is the best person for the job, that he is worthy of it. Then the rules will be bent to accommodate the change.

Take the case of Carol. She is junior-level clerk. She is performing the tasks of an absent first-level manager and is doing quite well. Her responsibilities include a few administrative tasks, many first-level managerial tasks, and an occasional second-level task. Someone inside the corporation realizes that this junior-level clerk is doing a first-level manager's job and alerts the department head. Carol has not yet become a *21* and does not know that she can be an exception to the rule. Her organization has one *21* in it. What do you think will happen if the rule states that only senior-level clerks can be promoted to management and Carol is one level lower?

This is an actual case. The *21* in the organization said that since Carol had distinguished herself in the job, she should be moved into management, even if the paper work had to be floated in such a way as to first make her a senior-level clerk and then promote her again. The *20's* said that only a clerk with more seniority could be promoted into the job, even if the person chosen lacked the skills to perform the task.

The absurdity of all of this is that the criterion, the rule, being used for making the decision is not the quality of the person's work but her level, a nebulous term and possibly the result of past hiring and promotional errors. If a clerk is doing a manager's job, doesn't he or she deserve a manager's title?

As this book goes to press, this problem is still not solved. It has lingered for months. The clerk is doing the managerial task and the *20's* are still unhappy. The only thing that has changed is that Carol has attended a coaching session on being a *21* and is in the process of making herself an exception to the rule.

You need to identify the rules that are keeping you from your goal and then identify the person who can grant you permission to sidestep the rule. The *20's* listed on the back of your *21* Worksheet

Chapter Five: The 21's

may help you pinpoint the rules that are causing you problems. As your list of *20's* grows, review it to see if there is a specific issue that keeps cropping up and needs to be addressed. If you must have specialized training to achieve your goal, then enroll in a class. If the opportunity you desire is in another state, then notify management that you are mobile and willing to relocate. As long as the reason, the rule, is valid, obey it. But if the rule is just for *20's*, find a way to become the exception to the rule.

Earlier in this book I told you about the time I had a solid business case for a new telephone service, proposing that for a $150,000 investment my company could generate $3 million over eighteen months. I was handed the same line over and over again. It could not/should not /would not be done because the president of the company had said that there would be no more special systems using nonstandard equipment. That was the rule. The rule was valid because manufacturing such equipment usually consumed a lot of resources, while special systems rarely returned much revenue. So because most special systems were not worth the effort, all special systems were to be refused. My business case showed that we were worthy of the exception to that rule and also showed that there was a tremendous payoff for the person who had set down the rule. I made myself an exception to the rule, and the special system was developed.

You must be worthy of the exception and there must be something in it for the person who has the power to bend the rule. In Carol's case, the benefit to the department head is that he will have recruited a manager who is proficient in her work.

> **You must be worthy of being the exception to the rule**

Know what you and your idea are worth. Thomas Edison had finally perfected his device which would later be known as the ticker tape machine. Since Edison was an unknown, he was afraid no one would pay him a fair price for his device. Also, Edison, who was twenty-three at the time, and was considered too young to be taken seriously. He mustered his courage and made a call on a customer, intending to ask $5,000 for the machine. At the last minute he lost his nerve. Instead of asking for his price, he asked the customer what he would be willing to pay. The customer offered him $40,000.

Do you know how much you are really worth?

A friend of mine, Wendy Keller, posed an interesting question. Wendy is a book agent, the person to whom aspiring authors send their manuscripts hoping she will then take the manuscripts to the publishers. She said that her job required her to reject more than 90% of the submissions she receives. She was genuinely concerned when she asked, "Does this make me a *20*? I am telling many people every day that I do not believe their idea, their writing or some element of their work is marketable."

One of the reasons we make a *21* Worksheet is to list those people who said our idea was without merit and why they said it. Just because someone writes a book does not mean that a particular publisher should publish it. It does not even mean that *any* publisher should publish it. The *21*'s know that sometimes they have ideas that are not as viable as others, and occasionally they have ideas that are not viable at all. I know I do.

Let's begin with the premise that for any venture involving another person, we must be able to answer one primary question: ***"Why is it in the other person's best interest that..."*** Whenever I want someone to do something for me, I begin with that question. If I cannot answer it, I seek the answer before I ask the person to do whatever it is I want them to do.

Chapter Five: The 21's

Let's go back to Wendy's situation. Someone has written a book and they want Wendy to spend her time, energy and other resources to promote their book. Why should she? The answer to that is in the question Wendy asks her customers, the publishers. She begins with the premise, "Why is it in the publisher's best interest that they take this book I am promoting?" When she can answer that question, the publisher will buy.

By experience, Wendy has learned what specific publishers will and will not accept. Publishers are interested in printing "marketable works". This means they want books that will sell. A lot of great books are not published because there is not enough interest to make the venture profitable. Some lesser books *are* published because the publisher thinks that a lot of people will buy the book. Therefore, Wendy looks for marketability, the same thing her customer is looking for, and the same thing the successful author will also seek.

So, Wendy comes into her office and there are the day's submissions. From all over the world, people have sent manuscripts that they are sure are the next best sellers. If Wendy turns them down, the authors may think she's a *20*. She begins reviewing the stack. Some submissions aren't even typed. Out they go. Others have serious writing flaws, grammatical errors and spelling errors. They are tossed out as well. There are a couple of romance novels in the stack; she does not represent that type of book, wrong agent, out it goes. Then there are the manuscripts for books with limited appeal like, "How To Teach Your Hamster To Fetch".

Each of these is rejected for a solid reason. If it were possible for Wendy to sit and write a letter to each of these authors explaining her reason for rejecting their work, the authors would know how to proceed next. Why should she? In other words, "Why is it in the agent's best interest that they send me a letter explaining why they rejected my book?"

Wendy Keller eventually finds herself with a short list of potential books, but the list is still too long. There are only twenty-four hours in a day and she can only professionally represent so many books. The short list contains the best of the batch; still not every one will make it into print.

She looks at one manuscript. It has flaws but it also has high potential. Working with this author will require a lot of her time and if she sees the potential for major payback, she may choose to take this project. This is why some people who are not as good technically have books published while other authors with stronger skills have their works rejected. It all boils down to, "Why is it in this person's best interest that they..."

If your *21* Worksheet is showing a pattern, act on it. If you are seeing the same basic reasons for rejection over and over, change what you are doing.

Follow this through. Wendy now gathers up all of the manuscripts she believes to be the most viable and heads to New York. There she will meet with the editors of two dozen publishers. Should the editors just buy her books? After all, Wendy is a seasoned agent, she knows good books, shouldn't the editor just take her word for it and publish the books? Of course not. The editors have to look at all of the manuscripts being submitted by all of the agents to determine which are the most salable. The editor will then reject most of the manuscripts submitted by the agents. Does this make the editor a *20* or a *21*?

The editor is a *21*. Even though they reject most of the works they see, they are still *21*'s. Sometimes the nature of the profession requires someone to say no more often than they say yes; that does not make them a *20*. The Broadway producer will audition as many

Chapter Five: The 21's

people as show up for a part in a play, only one will get the role. The football coach will look at virtually anyone who wants to try out for the team but only a certain number are permitted on the squad and only a few of those will be first-string starters.

Does this sound discouraging? It shouldn't. Go to your local bookstore and count the number of different titles on the shelf. Ask to see the book entitled "Books In Print" and see how many authors overcame the odds. Before the next ball game, watch as the players run out on the field. You will see how many of them persevered and overcame the odds.

In every case, the person who succeeds is able to answer the question, "Why is it in the other person's best interest that they..."

If you are a *21* and you truly want a critique, find the answer to this question. Would the agent send you a critique if you paid them? Would they critique your work if you offered to make a donation to the agent's favorite charity? In any case, the agent would have to be assured that once they gave you their critique, you would accept it and not end up arguing with them.

When I first entered the profession of speaking, I sent an audiotape of one of my presentations to a speakers bureau, a company that books speakers. I asked the owner, DuPree Jordan, to listen to my tape and give me his feedback. I promised to call him on my nickel at his convenience. I was sure he would say that I was the best speaker in the history of speakers. After all, that's what my friends were saying, that's what people said to me after my presentations.

Once on the telephone, DuPree said, "I'll give you a five minute critique. You're not ready yet. I think you have what it takes, you just need more platform experience." He then gave me a couple of ideas for improving my material and my promotional pieces and that was that.

Was DuPree Jordan a *20* or a *21*? Obviously he was a *21*. He knows what his clients are demanding and he knew that what he heard on that tape was not what his customers needed. Would the local Rotary Club hire me? Sure. But they don't pay. He understood what it took to compete with the best. Within a matter of months, he was booking me and he even occasionally sought my advice on some issues. Why?

Mutual respect is the answer. Come around to their way of thinking and the *21*'s will work with you, support you and encourage you.

The *21*'s will give you their ideas and their viewpoints and they expect you to respect them, even if they are wrong. *21*'s are not always right. I know a *21* who refused to invest in Coca Cola fifty years ago because he thought it was a fad. I know another who was convinced that eight track tapes would replace cassette tapes.

If many of the people you have contacted have said, the color is wrong, change the color. If they are telling you that you need to beef up some part of your idea, beef it up. If too many people have said, "You idea will be very marketable once this other event happens", wait.

What we are saying is, don't get hung up on the smaller issues. Our egos, as large as they may be, are always smaller issues. Don't let your ego get in the way.

> **Don't get hung up on the smaller issues**

How do you know that by doing this you are not just falling prey to the noise of the *20's*? The answer is in the consistency of the responses. This is why the *21* Worksheet is so important. *20's* rarely collude with each other to convince a budding *21* that they cannot,

Chapter Five: The 21's

should not, or will not succeed. *20's* typically grab the first objection they can think of and toss it out. Most people, too many people, take the objection as law and fall prey to it. This is what the *20* is hoping for, and it is not how you will respond. Instead, you will make note of why they are rejecting your idea and begin watching for a pattern. If the pattern repeats itself, there may be merit in the objection.

There are obvious exceptions, of course. Many *20's* pounce on obvious reasons why you cannot succeed. "You're a woman", has worked wonders for years. The implication is that since no other woman has even been that or done that, you, being a woman, can't do it either.

There had never been a female Secretary of State until Madeleine Albright took the office. How many *20's* had held to their long-term belief that only a man could hold that position? Can you imagine how many times in her life Madeleine Albright had been told her gender would hold her back? Others, in fact many others, had told her that her lack of education would keep her from attaining her goals, so she went back to school and continues to study feverishly. She had been told her lack of experience was an issue so, paid or unpaid; she got involved with one project after another. The legitimate weaknesses were addressed; the superficial ones were ignored.

Learning to sort out the noise from the *20's* and the legitimate issues we need to resolve is a lifelong learning process. It isn't easy, especially when someone who has proven to be a *21* in one area, turns out to be a *20* in another. Remember, Thomas Edison did not believe that airplanes and gasoline powered automobiles would ever prove to be commercially successful. IBM ignored or misread the potential for the personal computer and yet they are one of the most advanced and best managed companies in the world.

How can we avoid getting some of the negative feedback from the *21*'s? Here are a few ideas.

1. Involve 21's in their areas of expertise. My agent, Wendy, will reject any and every romance novel and science fiction work. This is because and only because these are not her areas of expertise.

2. Know your subject. Too often the *21* is approached with a "revolutionary new idea", which is in fact, an old and tired idea. There are some concepts that seem to get resurrected periodically. If the *21* has seen it before and the person with the idea does not know that it is an older idea, the *21* will probably reject it. *21*'s think that anyone pursuing an idea has done his or her homework. A dear friend of mine told me about his idea for a new book, one that had never been done before. I gave him the titles to several books already out and also the magazines that ran columns on the same subject. The only reason I knew these things is that I had the same "original" ideas years earlier only to learn that it was already being done. Do your homework.

3. Give the 21 a reason to look at your idea. Ideas are a dime a dozen. Even great, revolutionary ideas don't cost much more than that. Of all of the people asking for the *21*'s time, why should they allocate some to you?

4. Make it as easy as possible for the 21. Meet them on their terms, at their leisure. Two things will serve you well here: humility and patience. The *21* is usually more likely to spend time with the person who is seeking direction and looking for good counsel than they are with someone who has the greatest idea in the history of ideas, one that will make everyone rich and famous! It's a lot easier for the *21* to see merit in the strong yet humble individual. About once a month I receive a video, audio or a book that someone wants me to review. I simply don't have the time to review them all and, lacking any other motivation, I will probably ignore them. However, if the person calls in advance, explains their project and is willing to work around my

Chapter Five: The 21's

schedule, I will usually help them if I think I can. *21*'s want everyone to win, still, there are only so many hours in a day.

5.   **Thank the 21**. Whatever the *21* says, however they react, thank them. You have asked them for something and they have delivered something. Say thank you. Even if what they delivered was not what you wanted, even if it was the opposite of what you wanted, they have helped you. If you ask a *21* to review your proposal and the *21* says they are too busy, write them and thank them for their consideration. What they have told you is that they are not the person to help you right now. That thank you letter may also open the door the next time you want to involve this *21*. If the *21* says, "I have reviewed your idea and I don't think it will fly", thank them. They have taught you something. You may not yet know what it is, but they have taught you something.

It amuses me when the better *21*'s turn down my idea and then follow their turndown with, "Of course, I've been wrong before..." There is no one person who knows everything, no person who calls every shot correctly.

Know what you want

Know what you want. Know as much as possible about your idea, know what your idea is really worth and then act accordingly.

In business situations, the most powerful motivation for a manager is more business. For those of us in sales, this is a daily fact of life. The purchasing agent may not let us in to see the executive who would ultimately use our product because the executive has a rule that all salespersons go through the purchasing agent. This keeps the executive free from all those salespeople who are *20's*. I usually talk to the executive. How?

The purchasing agent has the ability to screen vendors from making appointments with the executive, but I have yet to meet a purchasing agent who has the authority to screen the exec's mail. As soon as the executive realizes that he is reading a sales pitch, however, he forwards the letter to the agent. So I write a letter that discusses the business problem and a solution that will bring more business to the executive and to their company. I don't mention product until the very end, and usually by then the person reading the letter is convinced enough to want to see and hear more - this time in person. They see the value to them: more business.

What you need from now on is a network of people who can help you define the steps necessary to achieve your goals. There must be value for them if you are to gain some of their time. *And you must appear worthy.*

Appearing worthy is a matter of image. What kind of image are you projecting? If you were an executive, would you be comfortable around a person like you? If your goal is to be a doctor, would a doctor see you as worthy of his or her time? Image is more than appearance or dress. It is also what you say and how you say it. It is an attitude that permeates the way you think, the way you walk, and the way you sit. As you make yourself the exception to the rule, make sure you appear to be an exception to the rule.

In our seminars on preparing college graduates for their entry into the marketplace, we stress the importance of their image and the impact that it will have on their future employer's first impression of them. It amazes me that many upper managers lose the sense of importance of image and try to regain it when they need to be an exception to the rule. Image management is an art that should be practiced throughout your career.

Chapter Five: The 21's

Can you recall a time when you made yourself an exception to the rule? Can you recall an instance when someone else did? How about the times you have gone to a restaurant that does not accept reservations and have been told that there are no available tables, only to have someone come in behind you and be seated? How about the person who can always find tickets to the sold-out concerts?

In business, do you repeatedly see the managers who seem to be the exception to the rule? The salesperson who constantly exceeds his or her quota is not subject to the rule that says all employees will be at their desks promptly at 9 A.M. That rule is for the *20's* who have to be managed as they try to not produce. Get the idea?

Now, back to the issue of why an executive or a public figure or any individuals who believe they are important would grant you any of their time. First of all, are you worthy of their time? Of course you are, but how do you tell them? Is there anything in it for them? There had better be, or you won't get to them.

Second, remember that their time is valuable and you must be judicious in taking any of it. Make your request for time as succinct as possible. This will tell the person that you can be brief and still convey information. Practice this request over and over until you are comfortable with it. You will have the ability to demonstrate that you are worthy of this person's attention - you have a need and you will not waste his time.

If you are a CEO or other senior officer in a company and you are approached for advice by someone who appears worthy (and sincere), how are you likely to react? Will your response be that of a *20*: can't/shouldn't/won't be done, violation of the rules of protocol, and so on? Or will you respond as a *21*: "I will see you for fifteen minutes on the third", or, "I cannot fit you into my schedule now, but if you will call Mr. Jones . . . "?

Winners, like *21*'s, know that everyone can teach us something. I have yet to meet the person who could not teach me something. In 1905 the world's largest diamond was discovered in a mine in South Africa. The diamond weighed - are you ready for this? - over 3,000 carats. That's about two pounds. It was discovered when someone literally stumbled over it. It was sent to England by ordinary registered mail. King Edward VII looked at it and said, "I would have kicked it aside as an ordinary lump of glass if I had seen it on the road".

21's are seeking people who can show them where the treasures are.

Occasionally I will see someone on television and ask myself, "If I had five minutes with that person, what would I ask them?" Prepared people seem to find more opportunity. It never ceases to amaze me that when I have the question ready, the person appears. I saw Henry Kissinger on CNN one night. He had been out of the public eye for years. Once I formulated a question for him, I found myself in a room with him. One Tuesday, a singer was in my office asking about how she could promote her new album. The next day Gladys Knight was sitting across the aisle from me on an airplane. After we landed I asked her for some time and carried her coat to baggage claim while she gave me a wealth of information that will help my friend.

And here's a quick word about truly successful people. Most of them, not all but most, are the nicest people you will ever meet. They are subjected to daily appeals from leeches and thieves.

> **Most truly successful people are some of the nicest people you will ever meet**

Chapter Five: The 21's

These are people who want to capitalize on the successes of others without having to bear risk or really work for it. These hangers on usually surround successful people and they treat them the way a horse treats the flies that hang around them. They let them buzz all they want and they swat them when they try to bite.

Gaining the advice you need to start out on your goal will probably be the first opportunity for you to use the Theory of 21. From then on, the process is the same: identify the person who has the information you need or who has to perform a task for you, and approach that person as someone worthy of their time and with a payoff for them.

Now rewrite your goal. Include the date that your goal will be realized and affirm that it WILL happen.

Here is a question that many people I interview cannot answer: In one sentence, can you define "success"?

You want to be a success, right? You know people who are successful, right? But do you really know what success is? If you don't, how will you know when you have attained it?

Success for you and success for anyone else are two different things. You will attain your success and you will live with it. So what is success? Some people tell me that success is a Mercedes, a big house, or lots of money, but those are the by-products of success. If your goal is success and success for you is a lot of money, there are plenty of ways to attain your goal and most of them will leave you feeling less than successful even when your bank account is bulging.

> **What is your definition of success?**

Before reading any further, develop your definition of success. Make sure it is clear in your mind.

Now compare your definition of success with your goals. Are they compatible? If not, then change the one that is out of place. If your definition of success is moving up the corporate ladder and one of goals is to coach a Little League team, these may not be compatible. Moving up the ladder may require a lot of after hours activities: dinners, seminars, going back to school, etc. The only way to know for sure that you are singularly focused is to work through this exercise.

Now LETS GO BE *21*'s!

Put together your *21* Worksheets, look at your target dates and strategies and tactics, and start out on your quest, NOW.

One final note about *21*'s: I am often asked if I believe that nice guys finish last, and if that's so, aren't all *21*'s "bad guys," since they finish up front? The answer is that it is true that nice guys finish last. It is also true that nice guys finish first. Being a nice guy does not determine where you wind up in the race, it only determines how you run the race. Being a *21* should have little impact on others' perceptions of whether or not you are a nice guy. *20's* may think that you are becoming snobbish because you are not spending (wasting) as much time with them as you used to, and there is a normal resentment that some people feel toward others who are successful. Be aware that some people may not appreciate *21*'s, but don't let that deter you from setting your goal to be one.

Believe it or not, almost everyone loves a winner. Be a *21* and be a winner. And be a "nice guy" about it all.

Chapter Five: The 21's

Want to make someone else into a *21*? Wouldn't it be great if everyone you dealt with was a *21*? Read on . . .

Chapter Six

Building 21's

God never created a Twenty. He made only *21*'s. *20's* are the products of mankind, and they have the ability to convert back to *21*'s.

There is within each of us a child - an innocent, malleable mind that entertains the impossible. It is this mind-set that permits *21*'s to be *21*'s. When this kind of thinking is buried under negative, pessimistic attitudes, the end result is Twentyitis. To make a *21* out of someone afflicted with Twentyitis, you must first push the negative thoughts aside to allow positive thoughts to enter. Once the thoughts are positive the actions will become positive as well.

I believe that every *21* has the responsibility to build more *21*'s. Some people have the responsibility of building *21*'s as a part of their job description. These people include teachers, managers, supervisors, and ministers - anyone who influences or controls the activities of others.

Every 21 has a responsibility to build more 21's

The single, most important function of management is to teach. If you are in any type of management position, you no longer have the choice of whether or not you will teach, you only have the choice of what you will teach. Will you build *21*'s or will you perpetuate the thinking of the *20's*?

If you watch children at play, you will see how they allow their imaginations to dominate their thoughts and their activities. Their uninhibited minds give them the attitude that almost anything is possible. At play, a child can be a doctor, police officer, schoolteacher, parent, or astronaut. This thought process bridges over into reality when children assert that they intend to be doctors, police officers or whatever when they grow up. They believe their goal is possible, and at that point in their lives, they are *21*'s.

Thomas Edison was discouraged by one of his schoolteachers from entering any profession requiring him to use his mind. The teacher even sent a note to Edison's mother declaring him to be untrainable. A high school football coach told Herschel Walker that he was too small to play the game and yet he went on to win the Heisman Trophy.

These are people who overcame the negative influences and continued to be *21*'s. But how many other young minds succumbed to the discouragement of the *20's*? We might have had the electric light and the phonograph sooner if some of Edison's upperclassmen had been stimulated instead of stymied. If their teachers had encouraged them instead of discouraging them, how much more would they have accomplished? Would they have reached their successes sooner?

Most teachers are *21*'s. Think about it - they spend their days telling their students what else they can do. They explain that they must learn today's lesson in order to understand tomorrow's lesson.

> **20's are honorable people – just misguided**

The motivation for the actions of the *20's* is often honorable.

Chapter Six: Building 21's

They are convinced that they are doing the right thing, based in part on their own experience as *20's*. The unfortunate part is that they are actually acting out of ignorance. They may be ignorant of a person's real ability and ignorant of the Theory of 21. For all their effort, they could just as well have stimulated their charge into maximum performance. Since you have read this book this far, you know that the potential for success resides within *everyone*. There is no excuse for us to discourage anyone.

But don't confuse the lack of discouragement with encouragement. If you are to make a *21*, you must encourage the person actively, not just refrain from holding him or her back.

Why would you want to encourage someone to become a *21*? What's in it for you? Those are the types of question a *20* asks, not the types of inquiries I expect from a *21*. A *21* knows why he or she wants to make another *21*: to improve the individual, to improve the company or other organization, even to improve the world. Everyone benefits from the successes of a *21*, even the *20's* who opposed the *21* initially. For instance, we all enjoy the benefits of Thomas Edison's work, and even those who told Herschel Walker that he'd never make it as a football player enjoyed watching him play football.

But the conversion process for reclaiming *21*'s can consume a great deal of time and energy. And since not every *20* is capable of change, the time and effort may yield no improved results. There are ways to improve your chances of success in converting a *20*, and there are ways to increase the likelihood of success.

First of all, understand who can and who cannot be made into a *21*.

> **Learn to determine who can be made into a 21**

It takes a lot of practice to be able to recognize the salvageable from the unsalvageable, but there are some signals to look for before taking on a

20 as a project. The Twentyism or Twentyitis must not be too ingrained, and the *20* must desire to be a *21*. There is such a thing as Terminal Twentyitis. There are people who will choose to live their entire lives as *20's*, never seeking or even considering a cure.

If the Twentyism or Twentyitis outweighs the desire to become a 21, or if there is no desire to become a 21, there is little hope of converting the 20 to a 21.

Tom came into sales as a *+20* and wanted to remain so. The only problem was that he was assigned to work for me. *+20's* can survive in sales, and occasionally, under the right circumstances, so can a *-20*. But I had no room for either in my organization, so I attempted to convert Tom. The first step would be to make him *want* to be a *21*, and the second step would be to convert him.

Tom saw the others in the group, all *21*'s, and saw the accomplishments that each had achieved. He also saw the honors and accolades that his peers were receiving. He wanted to be a *21*, or so he told me. It turned out that he wanted the accolades, but he did not want to have to live as a *21*.

I would give Tom projects, easy ones at first. As long as I was actively involved, pushing and pulling, he responded like a *21*. However, as soon as I handed over the reins to him, Tom reverted to being a *20*.

Tom brought me a problem and presented five reasons why a certain project could not be completed. We started with the first reason and mapped out a strategy and the tactics to overcome the obstacle. This first reason was a lack of equipment for the project. I asked Tom where some equipment might be found and what could be done to have it shipped to the customer's location in Miami by the due date.

Chapter Six: Building 21's

Once the synergy started, Tom became excited and began developing the tactics to overcome this obstacle.

By five o'clock that afternoon, after a few false starts and several trips into my office for reinforcement and encouragement, Tom announced that the equipment had been located and one more telephone call would make it happen and he would make that call the next day.

"Why not now?" I asked.

"It's quitting time," he replied.

Apparently the look on my face prompted Tom to make the call. But as he moved through the other four obstacles, similar symptoms of Twentyitis kept emerging. At one point the project was dropped for lack of a certain piece of paper. Another time the dead end was a person who would not return Tom's telephone calls. I thought that my motivation and Tom's mounting successes would cause him to become a *21*. I was wrong.

The due date was missed because at the last minute an old engineering friend of Tom's found another obstacle, and Tom accepted it. Despite his recent successes, Tom's desire to be a *21* was not strong enough to overcome his chronic Twentyitis.

And despite all of my efforts, Tom remained a *+20* and eventually had to be transferred to another department. His problem was one of continued exposure to *20* managers. Even after Tom saw and appreciated and even admired the accomplishments of the *21*'s in our group, the years of negatives would still take over and cause Tom to think and to respond as a *20*.

There are the *20's* who can be converted, and they come in all different colors, sizes, and shapes. They come from both sexes, all ages and every vocation. The only things that they have in common are that they are not terminally afflicted with Twentyitis and that they desire to be *21*'s. And you can help to instill the desire to become a *21*.

There is great value in converting a *20* to a *21*. There is value to the born-again *21*'s employer or other organizations they belong to: the new *21* accomplishes more for the organization. There is value to the born-again *21*'s family: the new *21* becomes a better spouse, parent, or sibling. And there is value to you for having converted the person: you have another *21* to help you accomplish your goals. But your having improved another person should be enough incentive for you to want to make more *21*'s.

Just as *20's* tend to propagate themselves, so do *21*'s. When you make a *21* you are starting an entire new line of *21*'s. To use a network marketing term, think of it as your "down line". These are the people you made into *21*'s who in turn built more *21*'s.

> *21's enjoy surrounding themselves with other* **21's**. *They relish the opportunity to convert a* **20**. *Henry Ford was a tinkerer when he became friends with Thomas Edison. Edison may have had the greatest influence on making Ford a* **21**. *Our choice of friends and mentors can often have tremendous effect on our ultimate success.*
>
> *Thomas Edison once asked a model maker to build a mock-up of a device he called a "phonograph". The model maker said it would never work. Edison smiled and said, "Build it anyway." Years later, Henry Ford asked one of his engineers to build a "shiftless" (automatic) transmission. The engineer*

Chapter Six: Building 21's

said it would never work. Ford said, "Build it anyway." Where do you suppose Ford learned that?

Remember that *21*'s are not people who lack the qualities of a *20* but people who possess the qualities of a *21*. There is an important distinction. As you achieve success in removing the negative thought process from a *20*, be sure that you replace it with the positive thought process. Simply eliminating the wrong type of thinking will possibly neutralize the *20* for a while. But if left unattended and without positive reinforcement, the person will revert right back to being a *20*. And even us born again, dyed in the wool *21*'s still have at least some smatterings of *20*-type thoughts. But we recognize them and immediately replace them with the thoughts of a *21*.

Making a *21* is a swap: the *20* gives up the negative and takes in the positive. It is a two-step process.

> **Making a 21 is a two-step process**

We live in an age of change. For this reason, we need *21*'s more than ever before. Can you name any field that is not undergoing rapid change? My doctor tells me that he can no longer keep up with reading the bulk of what is being written about his area of specialization, much less the entire medical field. My attorney pointed to a box of volumes and said that they contained the changes in the state law for this year. I can no longer do my own income taxes because of all of the changes in the tax laws. My mechanic must now know almost as much about my car as the person who designed it, and more than a design engineer knew just a few years ago. After all, the computer technology in my car exceeds the computer capability of the Apollo space module.

In the old businesses and in the new professions, change is encountered daily. Students entering specialized computer schools are being told that before they can finish their education some of what they learn will be obsolete.

There is no escaping the impact of change. *20's* believe that they can stall the change long enough for it to go away. They are mistaken. *20's* believe that things are still done better the old way, and again they are wrong. The opportunity to do things the old way, to block the inevitable change, and to assert that something cannot/should not/will not be done is becoming rare.

20's will not die a natural death. They will oppose new ideas down to their last breath. You will need the ability to convert *20's* to *21*'s for as long as you live. There will always be *20's* who will want to hold back progress. When they do accept change, they will do so reluctantly, slowly, a little bit at a time.

You determine who should be a *21* and decide that you will help mold him or her into a winner. If the person already wants to be a *21*, the first step is accomplished. If, however, the person does not want to be a *21* or does recognize the need to be one, your first step is to try to instill in him or her the desire to be a *21*. There are several ways to do this.

ONE

Be an example for the *20* to look to. I have found that almost everyone wants to be a success but few are willing to become a success. When they can see that an ordinary person is making it, they can begin to visualize themselves becoming successful, too. But they need guidance, they need a plan, they need you.

You can be an example in little things and in bigger things. Don't ever pass up an opportunity to be a *21* in front of a *20*. When you are

Chapter Six: Building 21's

with a *20* who you think has potential, look for opportunities to demonstrate the Theory of 21. Point out other *21*'s to the *20* and use them as examples. The *20* needs to understand that being a *21* is a way of life.

I was traveling in New York with a consummate *21*. We completed our work earlier than we had anticipated on a Friday. On the way to Newark airport he said, "Let's set a goal to be home in time for supper!" If you have ever traveled out of the northeast on a Friday you know how difficult it can be to find available seats. To humor him, the rest of us said, "Sure".

We went to a ticket counter and told the agent we wanted to be home earlier. The *21* pushed us aside and said emphatically, "We **must** be home in time for supper!" He had set a goal and now compromise was not an option.

The agent looked in the computer and said, "Every flight out of Newark is booked solid with waiting lists. You'd better keep the seats you have."

The *21* said, "You don't understand, we must be home for supper."

"There's no way you can do that out of Newark, sir", the agent said.

The *21* thought for a moment and asked, "Where would we have to be in order to be home in time for supper?"

The agent looked again and said, "Well, there's a flight out of Kennedy in forty minutes, that would do it. It's too bad you're not there."

The *21* said, "Book us on it and we'll go over to Kennedy."

The agent said, "There is no way you can get to Kennedy in time for that flight. If there was no traffic it would take more than forty minutes and this is peak traffic time. You'll never make it."

"We could if we had a helicopter."

"Yes, but you don't have a helicopter."

"Where can we find one?"

"Oh", said the agent, "In fact New York Air operates a helicopter service out of Terminal A. That's as far from here as it could be."

The *21* said, "You book us on the flight out of Kennedy and we'll do the rest".

With that the *21* took off in a dead run. He was twenty years my senior and had recovered from a heart attack and I couldn't keep up with him. We ran to the New York Air counter just as a helicopter was about to leave. We made the flight at Kennedy and also taught the other members of our team the value of being a *21*.

In great and small things, be a *21*. You never know who is watching and who is learning from you.

TWO

The second method is to tell the *20* that they can be a *21*. Some people don't know they can succeed because no one ever told them that they could. I know that sounds awfully simple, but I wish you could see the eyes of people who have never been told of their own potential until I tell them. It's usually the brightest part of my day! Most people have been told more times than they can remember that

Chapter Six: Building 21's

certain things cannot / should not / will not be done. They have accepted that as a fact, and for them it has become a dead end.

If you are in a management or supervisory position you must understand this. You have seen people who were not living up to their potential and you have wondered why. The reason is that you can see the potential and they cannot. Will you be the *21* who stretches them beyond their perceived limitations or will you be just another *20* in their lives?

Joe and I worked together as technicians. The company had agreed to assist the American Cancer Society in their drive to collect bed linens to be used in making cancer pads. The idea was that people would donate their old sheets and the cancer society would have volunteers convert them into something called cancer pads.

I never really understood what cancer pads were and still don't. I just knew it was a worthy case and I was happy to serve as the departmental representative for this project. Joe and I learned that the more affluent departments – you know, marketing, sales, engineering – would collect the most sheets each year. We decided to change that.

Joe was a budding *21*. We set a goal to collect 100 pounds of sheets. We believed in the goal and we started canvassing our fellow workers. After a couple of weeks we only had a small stack of sheets. Joe was losing heart.

One day over coffee we hatched a brilliant plan. We went to the shipping area and found a large cardboard box. It was over six feet tall and was about three feet on each side. Joe was something of an artist so he painted the box to look as though it was made of bricks. Then he made a door on the front so that the whole thing looked like an outhouse. He even cut a quarter moon on the door. In bold letters he wrote "Brick Sheet House" across the front.

The box generated a lot of curiosity and more than a few comments. It did not generate a lot of sheets.

We were getting close to the deadline and I was becoming discouraged. Then it dawned on me: who has a lot of sheets? People with lots of beds. Who has lots of beds? Millionaires (supposedly), hotels and hospitals.

I did not know any millionaires to call so I called a couple of hotels and asked them what they did with their worn-out sheets. Each of them told me that they did no have any sheets – they leased them from National Linen Service.

So I tried the hospitals and got the same answer: they leased their sheets from National Linen Service.

Who did I call next?

The gentleman at National Linen Services was a *21*. I asked him what they did with their old, worn-out sheets and he said that after they were cleaned they were placed in a bin and sold for rags (scrap). I asked him how much 100 pounds would sell for and he said they only sold by the ton.

I was almost too ashamed to ask how much a ton of sheets would cost, but a *21* never gives up.

"One hundred dollars a ton," he said.

Chapter Six: Building 21's

Then I asked if he would sell me a ton for one hundred dollars and he said something to the effect that anyone with that amount of money could take the sheets – he had more than he could handle.

I quickly grabbed Joe and we canvassed the office and collected the money. I called the man at National Linen Service and asked how to go about picking up my ton of sheets.

After some conversation, the man understood what we were doing and why we were doing it.

He paused for a minute and then said, "I'll tell you what, Buddy. Instead of you trying to find a truck, I'll have one of our trucks carry a load over to the Cancer Society. You send the money on to them – this one is on me."

See the whole picture?

Why did National Linen Service have so many worn-out sheets? Because their business was thriving. Why was their business thriving? It was because they had *21's* in key positions who were empowered to act like *21's*.

Joe and I both learned lessons on that one.

If you can influence someone who is a new or tentative *21*, use this opportunity to build them into a solid *21*. Whenever two *21*'s work together or even when they compete, the best in each of them emerges.

THREE

Still another method of convincing the *20's* that they have the potential to be *21*'s is by demonstration. The difference in setting an example and demonstrating is that demonstration involves explanation. We not only show what we are doing, we also explain how and why we are doing it.

When you have the opportunity, take a *20* aside. Show them something that you are accomplishing at the moment. Show them your *21* Worksheet or your strategic plan. Demonstrate to them that you know what you are going to accomplish and that you know how you intend to accomplish it. When my friend who became a general manager for A.T.& T. in San Francisco in his predetermined timeframe showed his plan to people, they became convinced that he would achieve his goal. When he showed it to his subordinates, and showed how he was on track with his plan, it demonstrated to them that they, too, could achieve their goals, and they would begin following his lead.

You need to demonstrate that being a successful *21* is not luck and is not a fluke. It is the result of planning and execution. If there is little or no apparent reason why you are succeeding, then the *20* is justified in thinking that your success is just luck. But when a *20* sees that you are attaining your goals through a systematic plan, it demonstrates to them that it is possible for them to attain their own goals as well.

FOUR

The fourth method is the most convincing: participation. Make a *20* a part of your plan, and the chances are he or she will emerge as a *21*. This participation can be as minor or as heavy as the *20* will allow. It can range from observation to total involvement. You can involve them in the planning or the execution stage. Involving the *20* also gives you the chance to use all of the other methods of

Chapter Six: Building 21's

proving to the *20* that they can succeed; i.e., you can now encourage them, inspire them through example as they participate in your plan.

I was a young technician with the telephone company and had been given the opportunity to demonstrate a new testing computer to some middle managers from around the country. Less than an hour before the presentation and demonstration, one of the managers involved with this show came into the room and asked me to provide writing tablets, pencils, and other supplies for the attendees. I had tried earlier to do that but had been blocked at the supply room by the supply clerk. There had been a rash of people taking such supplies (school was starting), and no one could have more than one pad or pencil. None of my explaining had any effect, so I had come away empty-handed.

I tried to explain all of this to the manager. Since he was a *21*, it sounded like nothing but obstacle noise to him. He handed me a telephone and told me to call the supply room and have them box up what we needed. I did, and got the response you might imagine. Then he told me to call the operations manager and explain the problem. I did, nervously, and was told that he would check on it and call me back. The manager went on about his business as if the problem had been resolved. The phone never rang, but five minutes later the supply clerk walked in with our supplies. I learned about being a *21* through participation.

Why did this work? The supply clerk had his marching orders, which were based on the assumption that people were misappropriating materials. This was true. However, a high level presentation to decision makers was an appropriate use of the materials. The clerk was not empowered to make an exception; the operations manager would quickly understand the situation and was empowered to change the rules. What was in it for the operations

157

manager? A great presentation to people who would be able to help him later.

Another kind of participation that can produce fast results is what I call the "deep end" method. One of my best friends and I wanted to learn to swim, so our fathers took us to the city pool. My father taught me the techniques of kicking, arm strokes, breathing, and the rest, and had me practice them over and over. My friend's father threw him in the deep end and let him learn, rather quickly, how to get out. The "deep end" method can be used when you need a quick conversion.

This is also known as the "artificial crisis" method.

Have you ever been in a crisis situation? Crises bring out the *21* in each of us, even if we've been accustomed to going along as *20's*. We find that we are able to accomplish the impossible and that we are able to do it expeditiously because we <u>have</u> to.

It amazes me that we prove that we can accomplish the seemingly impossible tasks when crisis strikes, but then revert to being *20's* as soon as the crisis passes. Why is that? Why will people stretch themselves beyond their limits to return something to the way it was, but will resist expending the same amount of effort to improve something? We see pictures on the nightly news of hundreds of people filling sandbags to stop rising floodwaters, working for days with little or no rest. Then we see city parks fallen into disrepair because the municipalities do not have the money to pay someone to do the repair work and the citizens don't care enough to volunteer.

The Theory of *21* explains this phenomenon by showing that most people are *20's* and that *20's* will expend whatever energy is necessary to have things remain as they have always been.

Another method, then, to encourage a *20* to become a *21* is to create an artificial crisis situation for him. Put him in a position where he must *do* something. Then, as long as he has to be doing something anyway, show him how to accomplish, not restore.

Stretch people beyond their perceived limitations.

Who is the manager or other person who meant the most to you in helping you become the success that you are? Were they people who stretched you beyond your perceived limitations or were they people who set the standards so low that you couldn't possibly fail? It was the person who stretched you, right? Now be that kind of a person. We may not appreciate the person who is pushing us at the time, but we do appreciate them later.

In 1966 I was drafted into the Army as the Vietnam War was approaching its peak. I got off the bus at Fort Benning and was met by a drill instructor. Over the next eight weeks he regularly stretched me beyond my perceived limitations. I didn't appreciate it at the time, but I really appreciated what he had taught me once I arrived in Vietnam.

As a manager, supervisor or influencer, ask yourself this question: *If you had to choose, would you choose to develop people who are happy or proud?* There is a level of happiness that comes along with "proud" that cannot be attained any other way. Be the kind of person that creates proud, not just happy.

An artificial crisis is any situation where a person feels that something dreadful will happen if he or she does not respond. Examples of artificial crises are production objectives, industry averages and sales quotas that appear to exceed the person's ability to achieve. Another artificial crisis is the deadline. The importance of any deadline can be exaggerated to the point that it becomes an artificial crisis.

I took over the account team and found that there had not been a true salesperson on the team for some time. There were two types of positions: account executive (sales) and market administrator (sales service). The account executive was a *20*, and after some effort I realized that I would not be able to convert him within a reasonable time, so I made my plan to replace him. The market administrators were all *21*'s and were right where they should have been, except for one. I determined that he should be the new account executive. He was selling, he was sharp, and his talents were being wasted in his current assignment.

I approached this person and asked him to accept the new position. He declined and gave as his reason the fact that account executives were on commission and his paycheck would depend on his ability to sell. Being an account executive would be a crisis situation for him since his wife didn't work and he had two small children at home depending on that paycheck. I asked him to think about it anyway.

Later, he said he had talked it over with his wife and he would stay in the lower position of sales service. I asked if I could talk to his wife.

As a sales service person he knew he was a *21*. But as a salesman he saw himself as a *20*.

In January this *21* became an account executive and his home, his house, his car, his boat were all riding on his sales. He was in a league with nearly a thousand other account executives and had a sales quota that was a challenge, to say the least. Many of the other account executives had years of experience in the job, but few of them considered themselves to be in a crisis situation. Experience had shown them they would survive. This account executive was not

Chapter Six: Building 21's

sure that he would survive, so, for him, this artificial crisis was quite real. As I said, that was in January. In September he received a letter from the vice-president congratulating him for being the number one account executive in the country. I was more proud of that letter than he was.

A classic example of managing *20's* and *21*'s occurred with the divestiture of the Bell System.

The Bell System was a hundred years old, had led the world in technology through its facilities at Bell Laboratories, and was providing the highest-quality communications service in the world. Independent surveys had determined that the company was one of the best managed in the world, even though it was the largest, with a million employees.

There was nothing wrong with the company, but the communications industry was changing. For the first time, Bell was facing competition. However, the competition was penetrating only the highest-profit areas, leaving Bell to try to compete while still providing service to the lower-profit users. In 1969 the Carterfone decision opened the door. Numerous lawsuits followed in the seventies, and it became *apparent to the brass at* Bell that change was inevitable.

There were the nay-sayers in the communications industry who said that Bell would never be able to compete because of all of the "dead wood" inside the organization. Since Bell was the largest organization in the world, it followed that it would have the most *20's*. Since many of Bell's efforts were almost totally regulated by local, state, or federal tariffs, the *20* mentality was functionally okay at the task level.

Following the Carterfone decision, Bell began mapping out a plan that would change the communications industry forever. For the plan to succeed, there would have to be *21*'s at all levels. Since Bell had never really had to compete, the first area of concentration was marketing. The executives at A.T.& T. developed and executed a plan to attract the finest marketers from IBM to the Bell System.

The sales force was analyzed, and a plan was developed to identify the *21*'s, build *21*'s out of the *20's* who could be converted, and make it easy for those who could not/should not/would not thrive in a competitive sales position to move into other jobs. A dynamic sales force was emerging from what had been considered the lackluster sales group of the old Bell System.

The new marketing guru used several tactics to achieve the strategy of building *21*'s out of the existing sales force by placing them in crisis situations. Since the existing sales force was divided geographically, he changed the lines of division to the customer's industry. Industry specialization became the order of the day. The salespeople were given the incentive to strive for the ultimate level of proficiency: industry consultant. For many of the old-time salespeople, this was a crisis situation. The game had changed entirely, all of the rules had changed. Those who could not change with the times simply left the sales department.

> **21's surround themselves with other 21's**

It was not essential, as some think, for the success of Bell that industry specialization be adopted. It was only essential that enough change be interjected to start the sales force thinking in a positive direction. If the existing organization had already been industry-specialized then the change to geographic dispersion would have been equally as successful, as long as it created an artificial crisis.

Chapter Six: Building 21's

The point is, there was a plan, the plan was being followed, and members of the sales force were being encouraged to become *21*'s.

Then the new marketer introduced "compensation," as the Bell System termed commission sales. Those who could sell and who sold more would be paid more than those who couldn't or didn't. This weeded out more of the *20's*. Those who could adapt to change but who could not commit to risking part of their salary to their ability to perform also left sales. These people saw compensation as a crisis.

Then the product line was scrutinized to determine which products were the most profitable and would continue to be the most profitable in a competitive environment.

All this time, the litigation and regulation continued. Less-informed people thought that Bell was missing the mark on some of the products and services. Some saw Bell as "sluggish." In fact, there was a plan, *20's* were being molded into *21*'s, and the plan was being executed. The litigation and the regulation could have created a real crisis had Bell not been planning around it.

The litigation was mounting. The Justice Department's lawsuit was into its sixth year and second judge. Congress was trying to enact a new Communications Act, since this high technology industry was still operating under the Act of 1935. More suits and litigants emerged almost daily. The water was coming to a boil, but would Bell be ready?

I was walking past the television department in a department store, and there on the screen were the chairman of the board of A.T.& T. and a representative from the Justice Department announcing that settlement had been reached in their lawsuit. Bell would divest itself of itself; the plan would be detained within six months and would be in the implementation process in less than a year. They were actually going to pull it off!

What amazed me the most about all of this was that the executives at A.T.& T. actually *thought* they could do it. Imagine the mind-set that entertained the thought that the largest corporation in the world, one with a million employees, over $60 billion in revenue, and billions in assets, could actually be divested to the satisfaction of the Justice Department, Congress, the customers and even competitors.

Most of us assumed that the original deadlines would be extended for a year or two, but we were wrong. Part of the plan included moving expeditiously as soon as an agreement was reached. This would again make *21*'s out of people who had not been severely challenged in some time. In less than a year a new company had to be born.

As the plans for the new company developed, some of the employees at Bell were given the opportunity to choose to stay with the regulated side of the business or move to the deregulated company. This was the ultimate weeding out of the *20's*, since *20's* saw a move to the new company as a potential crisis for them. Only *21*'s chose to move into the uncertain world of American Bell. Some *21*'s chose to stay with regulated Bell, for a number of different reasons that do not need to be discussed here. The point is that the new company, American Bell, was beginning with a large share of *21*'s in it ranks.

The original dates were met. In order to accomplish this, every phase of the beginning of the new company had to be expedited. This artificial crisis was the impetus that forced virtually everyone involved with the transition to act as a *21*.

Chapter Six: Building 21's

After American Bell was in place, the sales quotas were announced, and as you might expect, they were significantly higher than many people had anticipated. It occurred to me when I learned about these quotas that the marketing guru was still at it, still building what will be one of the strongest sales forces in this country.

Since this initial breakup, the communications industry and the former Bell companies have undergone many reorganizations and restructurings. The *21*'s continue to drive the changes; the *20's* continue to resist them.

I can tell you that few things in your life will be as rewarding as building a *21*. When you see the difference in a person who has learned that he or she can accomplish the impossible, when you see how it affects every aspect of this person's life, you will understand that the effort was well worth while.

You will also have another *21* to help you achieve your impossible goal!

Who is the *20* that you would like to convert into a *21*? Is it someone who works for you or reports to you? Is it someone who is important to you? Someone in your church or synagogue, someone in your civic organization? Or is it you? Identify the person, determine to convert them into a *21*, and then develop a plan. Sound familiar?

"I will accomplish the impossible goal of converting (NAME) to a *21* by (DATE). In order to do that . . ."

Here's another *21* Worksheet for you.

"I will accomplish the impossible goal of converting _____ to a *21* by _____.
In order to do that, I must first accomplish the difficult tactics of:

1.
2.
3.
4.
5.
6.
7.
8.
9.
10.

The tasks I will use to do that are:

1.
2.
3.
4.
5.
6.
7.
8.
9.
10.

Chapter Six: Building 21's

Here are my *20's*:

NAME   REASON

1. _____   _____
2. _____   _____
3. _____   _____
4. _____   _____
5. _____   _____
6. _____   _____
7. _____   _____
8. _____   _____
9. _____   _____
10. _____   _____
11. _____   _____
12. _____   _____
13. _____   _____
14. _____   _____
15. _____   _____
16. _____   _____
17. _____   _____
18. _____   _____
19. _____   _____
20. _____   _____

Chapter Seven

Types of 21's

There are six types of *21's*. The type of *21* you are and the type of *21* you need determines which one of these six types you need to approach. Asking the wrong type of *21* for help wastes time at best and can be detrimental at worst. We will discuss that in detail later; right now let's look at the six types of *21's*.

21's come in the following types:

1. Trackers
2. Hunters
3. Field Dressers
4. Chefs
5. Servers
6. Dishwashers

These titles were derived from primitive and modern terms that refer to our most basic need as humans: food. Primitive people learned to track down wild game and kill it. Typically, the eating began immediately after the kill. As man became more sophisticated, we learned the advantages of cooking the meat. As our sophistication increased, we began cleaning up after ourselves, spicing the food and even learning to garnish the meal. The basic need for food remains, what has changed is our process for attaining and consuming it.

In the same vein, ***21's*** have evolved over time to specialize in certain aspects of attaining another basic need: success. Let's look at each of the types of ***21's***.

Trackers

There are people who are experts at sniffing out new opportunities. They know where the opportunities are now and they know where the opportunities will be in the future.

Primitive man learned that animals left tracks and other indications of where they were headed. By learning to identify and follow those indicators, food was more readily available. The able tracker could find better food faster. This became increasingly important as the population increased and as the competition for available food became stronger.

The tracker learned that certain animals went to certain places during certain seasons, so they were the first people to operate on identifiable cycles. Some sheep and goats migrate to higher elevations in the summer to escape the heat and then return to lower elevations in the winter in order to find edible plants. The tracker could begin with this base of information and improve his effectiveness as a tracker.

Like his ancestor, the modern tracker has learned how to identify where the game is going. They can also identify cycles that tend to repeat themselves and the trackers use these cycles to make better decisions faster.

For instance, a modern tracker will see their market moving away from higher technology and moving towards higher levels of customer service. When they see this happening, they begin

Chapter Seven: Types of 21's

focusing more of their efforts on service and put less emphasis on technical issues. For the CEO, this means that they place additional emphasis on customer surveys, response time and service quality levels while allocating fewer resources for research and development. For the sales manager, this means that they focus their salespeople on selling the value of the ancillary services rather than specifications, features and benefits.

The *21* Tracker also knows that it will not be long before the emphasis will once again be more directed towards technical innovations and less towards service. They know how to track the cycles.

If you have an idea and you want to know where the idea will find the greatest possibilities for success, ask a Tracker. The other types of *21's* may not be able to answer your questions at all and, for sure, the answer of the Tracker will be more accurate and more useful.

There are fishing and hunting guides who are professional trackers. I have never really understood why these people do what they do. They take people out to the best fishing and hunting spots in the world, places where the absolute best in sport is found. And they never wet a hook; they never fire a shot. Their enjoyment is in finding the game, not hunting it. They are Trackers, not Hunters.

Dan Burrus is a futurist and the author of "Technotrends". He has learned how to look at the signs and determine where certain industries, markets, buyers and technologies are going. Once he sees where the business is going, he enjoys teaching others. Even when he sees opportunities with tremendous potential, he finds greater enjoyment in showing it to others than he does in trying to directly capitalize on it himself. He does not want to go through the details and "administrivia" of building an organization. He would rather be involved in the process of identifying the next opportunity. He does not want to be a Donald Trump, he wants to be the one who was paid by Trump to find the next great opportunity.

If your goal is to become an actor, the Tracker is the person who can tell you where the best roles are right now. If your goal is to be a designer, the Tracker can tell you which firms and industries are seeking designers and which firms are on the cutting edge. If your goal is to become a professional athlete, the Tracker will tell you which teams have tryouts and when the tryouts will be held. If your goal is to move up in your current organization, the Tracker is the person who knows what positions will be open, which are the most viable and what is required for you to be considered for one of those positions.

There are *21's* who enjoy finding the opportunities that others will address. They are successful in life because they recognize that their talent for finding opportunities is valuable to others; therefore, others will pay dearly for the Tracker's capabilities. Don't ask the Tracker how to land the opportunity - that's not their area of expertise. It is the specialty of the Hunter to land the big game.

Hunters

There are two types of *21* Hunters: Hunters and avid Hunters. The difference is their level of passion. In both cases, the Hunters spend their time following the Trackers. Hunters trust the information and assumptions of the Trackers. Based on the Trackers' input, the Hunters move the idea to the next stage.

The Hunter can land the game because they are <u>trained</u> and <u>equipped</u> to do it. Both of these elements are critical and both are dynamic, not static. Training is an ongoing process. New equipment is being

Chapter Seven: Types of 21's

introduced everyday and the better Hunters keep abreast with new technology and new techniques.

Hunters are in an ongoing training program. They never stop learning. There are two elements to training: education and experience. *21* Hunters read, attend classes and seminars, they are constantly seeking more information that can add to their level of education. The wise Hunter knows there is always something else for them to learn.

They also know that everyone they meet can teach them something. In the fishing camp and in the hunting lodge, sportsman swap stories. They talk about techniques they have learned or developed. They share ideas and everyone comes away wiser and better for the exchange.

Even while they are in the middle of a hunt, sportsmen will share ideas. Just as a golfer can improve their handicap by slightly adjusting their grip on their club, the game hunter can improve their results by altering their grip on their weapon. Sharing ideas, reading, being alert are all a part of education.

The Hunter also needs experience as a part of their training. As with any other physical endeavor, it is necessary for us to train the muscles along with the mind training. We need to develop habits of behavior in order to be the most effective and efficient in what we are doing.

I was trained as a soldier and was sent to Vietnam at the height of that war. My assignment had me in the field, or combat, for nearly a year. All of the soldiers and Marines depended on each other for survival. There were many occasions when we did not have time to think, only time to react. We needed to make sure that our reaction and everyone else's reaction was the right one. Our lives depended on it. Experience was essential. Our training had to involve countless repetitions of the most essential elements of combat in order for it to be a mental and physical reaction when needed.

We would spend our quieter times talking about faster ways to reload our rifles, better ways to sight an enemy target after dark and other techniques. We were trying to improve ourselves daily. Once the new technique was explained, we would practice it over and over. The training and practice helped us develop the habits that would determine our reactions, which would, in turn, determine our probability for survival.

After each firefight, we would critique what had happened. We would talk about how the battle had gone, how well we had been supporting each other, how well the artillery had backed us and what new techniques we observed the enemy using. This critique, or "post battle assessment" to use a military term, allowed us to capitalize on our experience.

We must experience new things and then learn from the new experience. To experience something new without learning something new is to waste time and effort. This does not mean that every new experience is a positive one. In fact, some of our best training experiences are negative ones. We seem to learn more from falling down than from walking upright all the time. Looking back on the experience, asking ourselves, "what did I learn?" and then critiquing it allows us to make the best of any experience.

Hunters also have the latest and the best equipment. You will find that the *21* Hunter is using tools and techniques that did not even exist a short time ago. They constantly look for new tools, and, when they find them, they assess them and determine how and when these tools can help.

Chapter Seven: Types of 21's

21 Hunters also keep the older tools in their arsenal. There are occasions when the older tool is actually the best and most appropriate one to use. Other times the latest technology is most appropriate. The bottom line is that the *21* Hunter has more tools today than yesterday and less tools than tomorrow.

For example, today's *21* Hunter knows how to use E-mail, satellite communications, multimedia presentations and other tools that did not exist only a short time ago. They also know how to write a basic business letter and how to make an old fashioned presentation. They know which people are most likely to respond to each approach and they use this information and these weapons on each hunt.

If your goal is to be an actor, the Hunter is the person who knows what each potential Casting Agent or Director is looking for and they know how to present you to that person. If your goal is to move up the corporate ladder, the Hunter can tell you how to present your accomplishments to each person you must convince.

Hunters believe in the principle that you must be able to answer the question, "Why is it in this person's best interest that..." They understand what the other person is looking for. The Hunter has the tools, the knowledge and the experience to make the hunt successful.

Watch the *21* Hunters. These are the people who are interested in landing the game, not necessarily in field dressing it. You will find that most entrepreneurs are *21* Hunters. They thrive on "bringing in another one". They enjoy starting companies, bringing new technologies to market and creating new organizations. They often do not enjoy running the business or perpetuating the new offering. As we like to say, they are in it for the "Thrill of the hunt". Once the game has been controlled, they want to move on to bigger and better opportunities.

Executive recruiters are Hunters. Executive recruiters are the professionals that corporations turn to when they need to hire people for significant assignments. Many of them take a job as a recruiter because they are unemployed at the time and they think that they will have access to a lot of new potential employment opportunities. What they learn is that they truly enjoy making success happen for others. There is a satisfaction that comes from knowing you have bettered someone else's life that just cannot be compared to other experiences.

The *21* Hunter is the person you will want on your team as you try to land your first success. They can help you understand what has to be done, how it can be done and what to expect. They are also abreast of the latest methods in hunting and they can often tell you about new approaches, ones you may never have considered. Once you know where your success is, after talking to a *21* Tracker, you will need the help of a *21* Hunter to move to the next level.

Once your dream, your goal, has been nailed, it is time to field dress it.

Field Dressers

In any enterprise, there is the start up phase. This is the time when the new opportunity is being closely examined for the first time. During this stage, the opportunity will need to be assessed to determine its long term viability.

Field Dressers start with a new idea and a blank piece of paper.

This is probably the trickiest time in the life of any new idea. Decisions made during this stage can affect the success of the

Chapter Seven: Types of 21's

venture for a long time. And yet, despite the importance of every decision during this time, there is precious little information upon which to make decisions. There is no track record for this venture and there may have been few similar opportunities in the past. Yet, this is a crucial time.

In game hunting, once the prey is felled, someone must move immediately to field dress it. Obviously, the game cannot be left in the field indefinitely - it will spoil or it will be taken over by vultures. And there is a right way and a wrong way to field dress the trophy. If the meat from the animal is to be consumed, one process is used. If the animal is to be mounted by a taxidermist, another process is used. There are some procedures that take place regardless of the intended use. For instance, some glands or organs in certain animals can begin secreting a rancid poison immediately. Whether you want to consume or display this animal, those parts must be removed immediately. So someone who understands field dressing needs to be involved as soon as the game is bagged.

A new venture is like the animal described above. We must assess its actual present and future values before we make our first move, and we must do it quickly. The vultures can snap up good ideas that are abandoned for any period of time. In business, vultures are those people who build their successes on the shortcomings and shortsightedness of others.

How we decide to treat this opportunity initially can make a difference in it being a long term or a short-term success. If the new idea is a fad, we need to treat it as such and field dress the idea for a short, hard run. If the idea is a trend, we need to field dress it for the long haul. There are *21's* who specialize in this sort of thing.

Here is where being a *21* gets really interesting. What if the *21* Field Dresser tells you to toss out part of your idea. Will they sound like a

20 to you? Suppose they tell you that after looking deeper into your idea, it has some flaws that cannot be overcome. Isn't that what a *20* would be saying? How can you be sure the Field Dresser is a *21*, not a *20* disguised as one?

The same rules apply to all types of *21's*: they must be dynamic, not static. They must be able to demonstrate a willingness and desire to continually update their skills.

The *21* Field Dresser is the person who can take your idea from concept to initial reality. As you talk to them listen for phrases like, "I was reading something about this the other day...", "I learned from a recent project similar to this that we need to...", or, "I will need to do some research on this to make sure I am up to speed..." These are all statements of a dynamic thinker, a *21* Field Dresser.

A *20* Field Dresser will say things like, "I have seen this before and...", "I've done hundreds of these...", and, "Been there, done that, won't work!" These are statements of a static thinker.

Many people dream too big. Many more dream too small. Very few of us dream at the right level. The *21* Field Dresser can do the best job of assessing the real long term and short term potential of your idea. You need this person.

Large and small decisions will be made. Do we buy a computer for the long haul or outsource what we need to have done on the computer? Do we sign long term or short term contracts?

Field Dressers do the initial preparation work for the new venture. They meet with other people, usually other *21's*, and develop new points of view. The *21* Field Dressers know who will give them a different perspective and whose perspective to trust. While they are field dressing the idea or concept, they continually update their understanding of its viability. If the opportunity seems to have limited potential, the Field Dresser will make what he or she can out of it, maximize the short term potential and move on to the next opportunity. If the opportunity proves to have tremendous potential, the Field Dresser will prepare it for the Chef.

Many entrepreneurs have brought in managers to help them grow their companies. These managers have an understanding of how entrepreneurs think, their strengths and their weaknesses. They know when the entrepreneur needs to be involved and when they need to back away. Typically, the entrepreneur brings in this manager and puts them in the position of Chief Operating Officer, President or some other high-ranking position. Usually the only person to maintain a higher position than this person is the entrepreneur. These "hired guns", as they are known, are the Field Dressers of high growth companies. They know they will take the opportunity from the embryonic, start up stage to the next plateau. They also recognize that when that time comes, they will leave the organization. This is why most Field Dressers ask the person with the idea for a piece of the action. They take equity positions in the new enterprise so that when the time comes for them to leave, they leave with more than a stack of paycheck stubs.

If your goal is to become an actor, the Field Dresser is the person who will help you be the absolute best you can be in the initial roles that will give you the experience you need for your resume. The Field Dresser in your town knows all of the people in the local art community, they know what is hot and what isn't and they can help you locally. However, if you demonstrate significant talent, the *21* Field Dresser will know that you are Broadway or Hollywood bound. These are areas where the Field Dresser has limited knowledge and experience. At this point, the *21* Field Dresser will introduce you to a Chef who can take you to the next level.

If your goal is to move up the corporate ladder, the *21* Field Dresser can show you all of the right moves in the local area or even in your region. To move into the big leagues, the *21* Field Dresser knows you will need a Chef who can maximize your potential. In most cases, the scope or the range of effectiveness for the Field Dresser is limited. The *21* Field Dresser knows this and recognizes when it is time for the Chef to step in. The *21* Field Dresser can make you a very successful middle manager. If they see executive potential in you, they will refer you to a Chef.

21 Field Dressers are the people who lay the foundation for the future success for other *21's*. Not involving one in your plans can bring about some unwanted results - even failure. Vanessa Williams had to relinquish her Miss America title because of some modeling she had done early in her career. A professional Field Dresser could have warned her away from such an unwise decision. Tim Allen made some, well, stupid decisions early in his career and wound up in prison. Both of these people overcame the early setbacks and succeeded but their lives would have been better if they had taken advantage of a Field Dresser.

In the movie, "That Thing You Do", the local rock and roll band has a hit song. A promoter, a *21* Field Dresser, appears and sees the potential of this group. He signs them to a contract and promotes them all over the state. One day the promoter introduces the band to an executive from a major record label. The band wants to continue working with the local promoter because he is someone they know and trust. The promoter knows it is time for the *21* Chef to take over and, in this case, the *21* Chef is the executive from the major record label.

The Field Dresser bows out when the Chef appears.

Chapter Seven: Types of 21's

Chefs

Just like the head chef at the best restaurant in town, *21* Chefs know many different ways of making the most of any opportunity.

My wife and I like salmon. It is full of vitamins, tastes good no matter how it is prepared and it is usually low fat. When we travel, we find new and different salmon dishes all over the world. We have had fresh salmon in Alaska and salmon dishes in London.

We have a favorite restaurant in Atlanta, Tom Tom's. The chef there is one of the most creative we have found. He recently added a new dish to the menu: salmon and grits. That sounds like something one would expect to find in rural mountain areas. In fact, it is quite a cosmopolitan entree. There is a salmon steak on top of a bed of cheese grits and the whole thing is topped off with the best cole slaw we have tasted. It is, in fact, the most popular dish at Tom Tom's.

The chef at Tom Tom's has used his experience, creativity, and understanding of the current market and capabilities of his kitchen to bring a new salmon dish to the table. This is how *21* Chefs operate.

21 Chefs take opportunities that others have started and make them grow. They may do this vertically or horizontally. Vertical growth is when the chef finds more ways to sell the idea to the existing customers. Horizontal growth occurs when more people begin utilizing the idea.

As an example, suppose you came up with a new software program. Your Field Dresser has worked with you in selling the software through advertisements in magazines and local newspapers. The product proves successful enough for the Field Dresser to recommend that you take your idea globally. The Field Dresser introduces you to a Chef.

The Chef takes your idea and your initial successes and begins building on them. Horizontal growth will come from making more people aware of the product. The Chef might be able to attract national or international advertising, alliances with computer manufacturers and other tactics that will put your software in more hands.

Vertical growth could come from upgrades in the software that allows the user to do more things or to do things faster or better. The same people who bought your initial software are now buying upgrades and enhancements. Another method might be for you to develop a home version of the office product, assuming your initial version was an office product.

21 Chefs are those people who know how to best capitalize on the better ideas. Like the Hunters, they keep an arsenal of tools and they continually update their knowledge and skills. They are on top of what it takes to bring about long term, solid growth.

If you have ever tried preparing a five or six course meal you can appreciate the difficulty of being a Chef. They will look at the new idea and they will begin to map out what will need to take place for the idea to grow to its fullest potential. They understand the complexities of the various functions that must be accomplished and they clearly understand the importance of timing.

The culinary chef knows that some things must be prepared in advance even though they will not be needed until much later. Some sauces, for example, require overnight refrigeration. Waiting until the day of the event to prepare the sauce is a recipe for failure. Other sauces must be prepared immediately before serving. This requires significant coordination. Every other aspect of the meal must be ready just as the sauce is being prepared.

Chapter Seven: Types of 21's

This is what the *21* Chef will be doing for you. This person will assess the long term viability for your idea based on what you have done, what you are doing and what else might be done.

In Denver, there is a company that pioneered data based marketing. Three entrepreneurs built the company using their specific areas of expertise. One is a software expert and was in charge of product development. Another was a master at sniffing out opportunities and was given the responsibility for sales and marketing. The third has strong administrative skills so he became the CEO.

The business thrived and grew. As it did, different people were brought in to capitalize on their specific expertise. After enough people were brought in, the company needed a human resources person. What a great problem to have!

The success of the company also attracted the attention of some competitors and would-be competitors. Lower priced competitors were penetrating the traditional markets into which the company had been selling. Meanwhile, the company was outgrowing its resources. The software expert brought in more people to help in product development. The sales and marketing guru built a streamlined sales organization. The CEO brought in a Chef, someone who could help them grow from an entrepreneurial company to the major organization they were becoming.

As often happens, a huge corporation watched their growth and then came in with a buy-out offer they could not refuse. The three initial principals walked away happy and successful people, the Chef stayed behind to take the company to the next level. Each of these entrepreneurs will replicate their success more than once.

Your Chef may be the person who teaches you the ways of the larger organization. Larger groups of people have to be managed differently. Trying to use what worked in the earlier days of your idea may actually bring failure later on. When the Chef says you need to make some changes, you need to make some changes. They are not being *20's*; on the contrary, they are taking you to the next level of being a *21*.

Is it difficult to discern who is a *20* and who is a *21*? Many times it is. But once again, look at the fruits of their works. Have they consistently produced winning ideas? After all, the Chef is the one player on your team who will be with you the longest. This is the person that continues to support your ideas and your projects. They teach you how to make the most of the new ideas you have as well as the new ideas of others.

Regardless of how good your ideas are and even if you are the most capable person in the world who is aligned with the best Chef in the world, you will still need support people to make your success happen. These support people are known as Servers and Dish Washers.

Servers

Think back the last time you went to a fine restaurant. Did you meet the chef?

The person with whom you had the most interaction was the server, the waiter or waitress who found out what you wanted and saw to it that you got it. Servers do not make decisions, they implement the decisions of others and they are capable of doing it very well.

Servers do not decide what will be on the menu; the chef does that. The server does not decide which restaurant the customer will patronize nor which entree will be ordered, the customer does that. Where servers excel is in finding better ways of meeting the demands of others and doing it in such a way that everyone is pleased.

Masters of coordination and administration, Servers are those people who take the limited amount of information provided by the other *21's* and convert them into practical, usable daily tactics. Erroneously referred to as the "people behind the scenes", these *21's* are the ones that will take your idea from concept to reality. Until we reach the task level, nothing really happens.

The Chef and Field Dresser can show you what must be done at various stages, they can tell you who to contact and they can give you direction. Until something is done, the person is contacted or some other activity takes place, nothing actually happens. You are only one person and, therefore, can devote only one man-hour of activity each hour. What would happen if you added someone, like a Server? You would now have two man-hours of activity each hour but the output would equal having three or four people.

The Bible says, "One can put hundreds to flight but two can put thousands to flight". There is a synergy that develops when we involve others in our activities. Ideas breed off of each other, energy increases and morale goes up. Knowing you are not alone and totally responsible for every aspect of your success gives you breathing room and makes you significantly more effective.

When my company was only a year or two old, my part time helper resigned suddenly. I was desperate. Asking around for someone to help a fledgling company, I was introduced to Debbie Orr. On her first day on the job, I gave her a one hour tour, explained what each pile of papers was for (my style of office management), what to say when she answered the phone and then I promptly left town for a few days.

When I returned from my trip, she had organized the piles into files (which were actually in drawers!), had handled some long overdue correspondence and documents and, generally, had everything ship shape. Over the next few weeks, she took on more and more responsibility and the business thrived. We added more staff as we grew and some of the hiring decisions I made weren't that good. She took over the hiring.

A few years later, we took the company on a different course. She modified her role, allowed us to downsize and, once again, the company thrived. Debbie is a *21* Server. She was on the front lines in communicating with the customers. She was on the front line with the vendors, maintaining inventory and resolving disputes. All of her efforts freed me up to do what I do best, which is write and speak.

This *21* Server does not want to speak in front of an audience - the idea is actually repulsive to her. She does not want to write books but she writes the best business letters I have read. *21* Servers know their strengths and they know the weaknesses of those around them. Not only will they take on the arduous tasks that too many *21's* ignore or do poorly, they also look for more ways to serve. I believe there were days when Debbie wondered how I was able to function and other days when she pitied my ineptness in certain areas. She always expressed appreciation for what I did and those compliments were always returned.

This the type of *21* Server you want to find. Look for someone who is strong in your areas of weakness, someone who believes that the impossible can be done and someone who will seek additional responsibilities. The purpose of the server is to allow you to do those things you do best by doing the things they do best.

Replacing Debbie was difficult. I panicked when I realized she was leaving. Still, we were able to find Karen White who has the same

21 attitude. Shortly after coming on board, Karen demonstrated her powerful organizational skills by developing and implementing several new systems that were needed more than I had realized. The *21* Server finds new ways to do things better. Listen to them and learn to trust them.

Dishwashers

In fact, there are people who are behind the scenes - the dishwashers. Customers never see or hear them, they seek little recognition and yet they are as vital to the success of any endeavor as anyone. These people take their jobs seriously because they know the value of what they do. In fact, the person behind the scenes often has a better understanding of their importance than the people in the public eye.

You will need as many *21* Dishwashers as you can find.

I was asked why I use the term Dishwasher instead of say, pastry chef or salad maker. After all, these are also behind the scenes positions and they carry more prestige. The reason I chose dishwasher is because of something I read recently.

We have commonly assumed that if someone was incapable of any other task, they could always wash dishes. In fact, dish washing has become another trade to succumb to high tech. Increasing sanitation requirements that are being forced on restaurants by government agencies and insurance companies. Some enterprising *21's* have seen this as an opportunity to develop automated, high tech equipment that will maximize the cleanliness of the dishes in the restaurant. Operating this equipment requires someone who is educated and capable.

I also selected dishwashers because I have some experience in this profession. Among the many other jobs I have had in my checkered past, I have washed my share of dishes. I know what it means to stand behind a large stainless steel sink, scrape dishes and then feed them into a sterilizer. This was during a time in my life when I was content to be one of the "unsung heroes", a person behind the scenes.

If dish washing now requires an increased education and more capabilities, how much more will be required of any success you are seeking?

Part of my work involves producing videotapes. When someone compliments one of my tapes, I know they are complimenting people they do not even know exist. For instance, the audio track on videotape will make or break the quality of the production. At every shoot there is an engineer who wears headphones virtually all day long. They hear everything. They have stopped our taping because a truck backfired a half a mile away or because the microphone barely brushed my shirt.

There are video editors who can make changes in the video effects that I cannot even detect. Yet it is this attention to detail that causes even the most ignorant person to see the quality in the finished tape.

The next time you go to the movies, watch the credits at the end of the picture. You will see a handful of names listing the people who wanted to be seen publicly - the actors. Then you will see list after list of people who choose to ply their trades behind the scenes. The movie simply cannot exist without the talents of these people.

There are many of these behind the scenes people at the base of every successful person. *21's* know that there are people who thrive on supporting the efforts of others. It is puzzling to many why

Chapter Seven: Types of 21's

anyone would want to do a lot of hard work, use their incredible skills and not seek public acclaim. Of course, it is just as bizarre to them that the rest of us want to be in the spotlight.

The *21* Dish Washer will be as proud of their work as anyone. I was at a man's house when we went inside to get some water. He took two glasses from the cabinet, filled them with water from the tap, held them up to the window and said, "I made that this morning." He is an entry level employee at the water department. He is a *21* Dish Washer because he is proud of what he does. He is proud of what he does because he knows he does it well.

No matter what your goal is, you will need each of the different types of *21's* to help you. Do not try to make your success happen alone. There is so much more that you can accomplish when you involve other people: two people can accomplish the work of several, other people bring us new ideas and, no matter what you are facing, someone has faced it before so why reinvent the wheel?

Hybrids

There are some *21's* who can actually function in more than one role. These people are known as hybrids. These are usually people who have been one type of *21* for a while and have now decided to develop the skills to be another type.

Hybrids are usually adjacent types, that is a Tracker-Hunter or a Hunter-Field Dresser. You rarely find a hybrid who has skipped over a type, such as a Tracker-Chef or a Field Dresser-Dishwasher.

Since the types of *21's* typically work with the other types of *21's* closest to them, they learn what is involved in being the other type. For instance, the *21* Hunter is often referred to a budding *21* by a *21*

Tracker. As a result, the Hunter begins to learn something about how the Tracker operates. Also, the Hunter refers budding *21's* to *21* Field Dressers because the Hunter knows what needs to be done next and they know that Field Dressers can make the next stage happen.

This typically happens when the *21* finds the need or desire to try something different to be very strong. The entrepreneurial *21* Field Dresser may help several companies in their start up days. After a while, that same *21* may decide that changing companies frequently is no longer as desirable as it once was and longs to have a more permanent position. As a result, this *21* may seek a position as a Chef in order to have a longer run with some organization.

Sometimes the game changes and the *21* determines that he or she would rather learn how to be a different type of *21* than to seek another assignment in their current level of experience. When a company begins outsourcing a certain function, the *21's* who have typically done that function will make a decision. Either they will seek another organization where they can use their existing skills or they will develop new skills that will allow them to stay with the same company.

Whether the motivation for changing is *want* or *need*, the *21* willingly makes the changes that will make their success happen.

Examples

Let's go back to Wendy Keller's question. You will recall from a previous chapter that she is the agent who represents authors who are trying to sell their books to publishers. She was concerned that she might be a *20* since she rejects far more projects than she accepts.

Chapter Seven: Types of 21's

Here is the question: Is Wendy a Tracker, Hunter, Field Dresser, Chef, Server or Dishwasher? She is a Hunter - she hunts for the right publisher for each project. Once she has found the right publisher, the project is turned over to an editor who is a Field Dresser. To really understand this concept, let's follow a book from conception to bestseller.

An author produces a manuscript and wants to make it into a best seller. Which type of *21* should the author contact first? The answer, of course, is the tracker. The author needs someone who can tell if the manuscript is viable, this person is the Tracker.

M. Kay DuPont is a Tracker. She is the author of the book, *"Don't Let Your Participles Dangle In Public"*. From the title you know she is a fun person to work with in refining a manuscript. Kay is the person who can look at the author's work and make suggestions and recommendations for improving it.

It is much better to have a Tracker tell you that your writing needs work than to have an editor or agent tell you. Why? Because once the agent or editor see bad writing from a person, there is a natural inclination to associate the name with bad writing. First impressions can be lasting ones. Why start out with a weak first impression with a Hunter or Field Dresser when a Tracker could have prevented it?

When Wendy Keller receives a manuscript form someone who jumped over the Tracker *21* and went straight to the Hunter *21*, too often the manuscripts is rejected even if it contains good, salable ideas. What a shame.

Some writers even jump over the Hunter and go straight to the Field Dresser, in this case the editor at the publishing company. In fact, so many people have sent unsolicited manuscripts to publishers that most of them now refuse to even look at them. There only viable way to manage the volume of unsolicited proposals is to send form letters to the authors.

Sometimes the authors think that the publishers are all a bunch of *20's* since they routinely reject so many submissions. The truth is that the author is the *20* for failing to make the best use of the resources at hand.

Who are the Chefs in the publishing industry? The designers, printers and marketers are. The cover of a book can dramatically influence the sales of the book. Designers have to know what is hot, what the target market for the book will be looking for and how to attract the eye of the potential buyer. Printers keep up with the latest technology for putting ink on paper. This may sound simple to people outside of the industry, but printing has become a high tech, rapidly changing science. Then there are the distributors who not only make the books available to the retailers, but they also make the retailers aware of new titles, which ones are moving, which ones will be promoted and other factors that the retailer needs to know to maintain the proper inventory levels.

The designers, printers and distributors do not want to spend their lives dealing with authors or editing manuscripts. They want to do what they do best. If you want to know something about book distribution, don't ask an agent or an editor. They know something about the subject but the distributors know everything about the subject. Ask an agent to help you distribute a book and they will say no. They aren't being *20's*, they are being *21's*.

The Servers are the retailers who sell the book. My wife is an avid reader. She will occasionally go into a bookstore and come away empty handed. Her usual method is to approach an employee of the store and ask if any of her favorite authors have published any new

Chapter Seven: Types of 21's

books. She will ask if the employee knows of other authors who write in the same genre. The retailer is the Server.

The Dishwashers are those people who are quietly recommending the book to their friends. They may even buy a copy and send it to someone. These dishwashers are not seeking recognition or reward, necessarily; they are trying to help others experience something they found enjoyable.

In virtually any profession or any endeavor, you will find the six types of *21's*. In the speaking profession, there is a great Tracker in Dallas, Texas. Her name is Juanelle Teague. She helps people refine their presentations skills, develop their marketing plan and create their initial materials. She can do this effectively because she was a Chef in the speaking business for many years - she produced seminars. In her life as a Chef, she learned how to find speakers, so she was a Tracker. She had to put together speaking contracts that were mutually beneficial, so she acted as a Hunter. With this background, she is able to be very effective as a full time Tracker because she knows what the Chef is seeking.

Another example

Customer Insight Company in Denver was founded by three *21's*, Randy, Ed and Nick. Ed was responsible for the administrative and soon realized he would need another *21* to help him so he brought in Tery. The company grew and was such a success that a major corporation came in and bought the company from Randy, Ed and Nick and left Tery in place as president. What would happen to these four *21's*?

Ed started another company. Randy went into semi retirement and does some consulting and speaking. Nick went looking for other opportunities.

Tery stayed behind and remained as president even as the company grew exponentially. I assumed that Tery was becoming a hybrid and was changing from a Field Dresser to a Chef. I was wrong. When I met with Tery he explained that Customer Insight Company was still as aggressive and almost as agile as ever. He felt he was still in the entrepreneurial phase since their growth year over year continued to be thirty and forty percent. If the company ever reached the point where Tery was forced to run a slow growing, mature organization, he would move on. He wants to be a Field Dresser.

Where are you in your quest for your success? Have you already identified the first steps you need to take? Then you may not need a Tracker, maybe you can begin with a Field Dresser. Have you gotten your idea underway? Maybe it's time for a Chef to advance your idea further. Who are the Servers, the people who are presenting different aspects of your idea to other people? Who are the Dish Washers, the people behind the scenes who are helping you?

I have not met any self-made successes. Every successful *21* I know attributes their success to the help they received from others. We all get by with a little help from our friends - especially the *21's*.

The Rest of the Story

As I said earlier, I was content to be a supporting player for a number of years. I am what is known as a late bloomer. Not until I was well into my thirties did I ever move beyond entry-level positions and support tasks. Inside, I knew I wanted to be more - maybe that's your story. You are proud of what you do and you do

Chapter Seven: Types of 21's

your job better than most other people. Still, there is a nagging that seems to be urging you to bigger and better.

I had been with AT&T for ten years when a **21** manager called me into his office. He said he saw more in me than I saw in myself. Those were not his words but that was his message. He suggested that I try sales. There was no way I was going to be a salesperson. My opinion of salespeople was not very high, so that would be my reason for refusing the move to sales.

The truth is that I believed, really believed, that there was no way I could ever sell anything to anybody. I was too shy and introverted to speak in front of groups. Powerful people like customers intimidated me. And - this was the big one - I lacked the necessary education. I had spent a year at the University of Georgia proving to myself and everyone else that I could not work two jobs and pull in good grades. Learning from books was very difficult for me.

The **21** manager believed in me and I believed in him so I took a shot at sales. My first full year in sales I was AT&T's top salesperson out of 1,100 salespeople. The company was so impressed they made me a sales manager, gave me the dead last account and nine months later it was number five out of 256 national accounts. Then I left to become a professional speaker.

I tell you this story for one important reason: you can be anything you want to be. If you want to be a career support person, you will never find a more supportive person than me. I have been there and done that. I admire and respect every person who enjoys what they do and do it well.

But if you have burning desire to be more than you are, then decide which type of **21** you want to be and begin the process of becoming it. If your heart is telling you to be a Server, be the best Server in the history of time. If your heart is telling you to be a Chef, do not rest until you make that a reality.

Don't settle.

Become your dreams. This is not a you-can-do-it message, it is a "you MUST do it" message. You must become your dreams for yourself and for others. Your real potential must be met for you to feel truly fulfilled. After all, God created you for a purpose and when He did, He also planted the seed of desire for that purpose within you.

Become your dreams for others. When I meet someone who works in a cotton mill, I empathize with them. It is empathy, not sympathy, because I have worked in a cotton mill. When I meet a Vietnam veteran who is struggling with posttraumatic stress syndrome, I empathize with them.

You have your story; you have your experiences. As you move towards your dream you will find many opportunities to inspire, help, lead and change those people with whom you empathize. You will be able to reach people that I cannot. In fact you will be able to reach people that no one else may be able to reach.

If you stay in a position where you do not belong, you hurt yourself and you fail to help the people you could have reached.

Do you understand the importance of becoming your dreams? Which type of *21* do you need right now?

Chapter Eight

Spiritual Justification

God never made a Twenty.

God does not create anything that lacks potential.

It is always God's desire – and His great delight! – that everyone be successful.

If you are wondering how The Theory of 21 squares with the Bible or other scriptures, here are my thoughts.

The Judeo - Christian ethic is loosely based on those areas where Christians and Jews agree. Much of the Old Testament in Christian Bibles is also contained in Jewish writings as well. It is difficult to argue with the Wisdom of Solomon as presented in Proverbs or the conclusions of David the Psalmist. I am too unfamiliar with the doctrines of other religions but from what I understand, most are founded on similar principles. So let's look at the Old Testament for an idea of how the Law might have been applied.

The Children of Israel wandered in the wilderness for forty years. They were heading toward the Promised Land, a "land that flowed with milk and honey". This was the ancient term for "the best of everything". In other words, this what a *21* would seek. It was called the Promised Land because God had promised it. That's important and we'll come back to it later.

The Israelites were held as slaves under the Egyptians prior to their nomadic roaming and God used several miracles to convince the Pharaoh to let the Israelites go free. Once free, the children of Israel, as they were known, repeatedly gave up. They would experience a miracle and soon after, they would give up. "Did you bring us into the wilderness to die? We were better off as slaves", became their almost daily mantra.

Their leader, Moses, was a *21* who had surrounded himself with other *21*'s. I don't know about you, but after the burning bush, twelve plagues, a column of fire at night, a cloud during the day and a parting of the Red Sea, I would think everyone would be a *21*! Not so.

If you will read the stories in Exodus, you will come across a *21* named Caleb. Caleb was a spy. Moses sent fourteen men into the Promised Land to scout it out. Twelve came back and reported that there was no way the Israelites could go in. The people there were giants, they were well armed and entrenched and they would easily wipe out any forces the children of Israel could muster.

Caleb and one other said it was possible. Where others saw imminent and complete defeat, he saw opportunity. Was this blind optimism?

There are several factors at work here. One is that Caleb served under a *21,* Moses. When we are aligned with another *21* or other *21*'s, we have a certain confidence that is lacking when we do not whole-heartedly believe in the person we are following.

The most significant factor, however, is that Caleb understood that this was God's purpose. It was God's purpose for him and it was God's person for the Children of Israel. He had witnessed other miracles as had the masses, but he had also learned the reason behind the miracles.

Chapter Eight: Spiritual Justification

There is a purpose for your life, God is behind it and if you are not already aware of the miracles He has performed in your behalf, some reflection might bring them to light.

What about the person you just happened to meet? The article you just happened to read? A lot of people saw apples fall from a tree, but Newton was prompted to ask why. Many people have met the person who gave you the idea or the information you needed, yet they came away without it.

Caleb saw the challenges to possessing the Promised Land and he also saw the rewards. He understood the potential for defeat and his experience convinced him that defeat was not inevitable.

Everything that has happened to you so far has happened for a reason. It was to teach you something. Some people never learn the lessons - they are *20's*. Some people learn the lessons and move on to the next one - the *21*'s.

Every lesson will be harder than the last, or at least it will seem that way. Being a *21* does not seem to get easier, only more difficult. The reason for this is that the *21* takes on greater and greater challenges. Having an audience with the person who help me was a real challenge the first few times I tried it; now it is a much simpler matter. Overcoming the objections of the *20's* was a real effort initially, now it isn't as much of a bother.

You and I are reaching for higher and higher goals. Once we have attained what we want, it is time to make sure that we are seeking God's purpose for our lives. No matter what we can imagine, He has greater on His mind.

So, until this moment, learning to be a *21* has been elementary school for you. Now it's time for the advanced courses.

Decide what you want by learning what God wants for you. Declare it to be yours. Then move ahead in your vision.

Are You A 21?

The Theory of 21 Test

Answer the following questions as openly and as honestly as you can.

1. You are one of three people being rated or judged for something that is an important area for you. It could be a promotion at work, an office in the local civic club or a role in a play. When the results are in, you are number 2.

- ☐ How do you feel about the person who was selected as number one?
- ☐ How do you feel about the person who was selected as number three?

2. What are your strengths? List the five traits or skills that are your strongest. These are abilities you have that you use everyday, such as the ability to meet new people, the ability to listen, computer skills, etc.

1. _____
2. _____
3. _____
4. _____
5. _____

3. For this question you will need a photograph of yourself from at least five years ago. Looking at the picture and looking in the mirror, answer the following questions.

- ☐ How does the hairstyle compare in the photograph and in the mirror? Worse Same Better
- ☐ How does your style of clothing compare? Worse Same Better
- ☐ How does your physical appearance compare? Worse Same Better

4. List the three goals that are most important to you right now. These are the goals that you focus on virtually every day. If you do not have specific goals, move on to the next question. Once you have written out the goals, answer the following questions.

- ☐ How many of these goals are ongoing goals? Ongoing goals were goals a year ago or several years ago.
- ☐ How many of these goals will require significant change, education or training in order for you to accomplish them?

5. A person you admire and respect has just achieved some significant success - something you have been trying to accomplish for years. What will you say to them the next time you see them?

6. A person you loathe has just gotten the promotion or position you wanted. What will you say to them the next time you see them?

Are You A 21? The Theory of 21 Test

7. The car in front of yours flips over, catches fire and traps the driver inside. You are married and have three small children. Which of the following best describes how you would react:

☐ You would attempt a rescue despite the potential danger

☐ You would call for professionals to help and in the meantime try to keep others from getting injured

☐ You would move out of the way to allow more room for emergency vehicles and personnel

8. You have reserved your favorite table at your favorite restaurant for a dinner with some of your friends. The person who arrived minutes before you demands "that table" and is seated at your favorite table. Do you...

☐ Demand that the manager move the other party

☐ Say to the manager, "I see that my favorite table is unavailable, what else do you have?"

☐ Leave and vow to never return to that restaurant again

9. You and your spouse saved for years to have the cruise you have always wanted. Due to a mechanical malfunction the ship misses a port of call. How do you react?

10. List the ten most significant things about your last vacation.

11. Someone is bragging about something they have done (a game of golf they shot, a fish they caught, a major sale they made, etc.). It is obviously an exaggeration. Do you

☐ Nod enthusiastically and congratulate them?

☐ Tell an even better story to hold up your end of the conversation while not making a point of their obvious exaggeration?

☐ Politely express disbelief?

THE ANSWERS

1. You are one of three people being rated or judged for something that is an important area for you. It could be a promotion at work, an office in the local civic club or a role in a play. When the results are in, you are number 2.

- ☐ How do you feel about the person who was selected as number one?
- ☐ How do you feel about the person who was selected as number three?

If you and two other people are being compared and you come in second, there are some clues about how much of a *21* you are based on the way you respond.

First of all, how do you feel about the person who was chosen as number one? If your response was something like this, you are a *21*. "That person knows something that I don't know or they are able to do something I cannot do. I will learn how to do whatever it is or I will learn what they know. Next time I will win".

The *+20* will respond with an answer like, "I was just as good - they probably kissed their way to the top". Or, they had to do a lot of things I wouldn't do, like spending time away from their family. My family is just too important to me". In fact, *21's* are usually great family people. They have learned how to bring balance into their lives. *21's* don't see as many "either - or" situations. When asked if they would like to be the best at something or be a good family person, the *21* answers, "Yes", meaning they will be the best and they will be a good family member. They will find a way to accomplish both. Attaining one goal does not preclude attaining another for the *21's*.

The *-20* responds with an attitude like this. "They just got lucky. I did everything they did, they were just in the right place at the right time. I will continue doing what I have always done and, sooner or later, others will appreciate what I do". *21's* know that doing something different requires doing something different. In other words, if I want to do something different like be recognized as number one, I need to do something different - something other than what I am currently doing. The *-20* typically expects everyone to come back to the old way of thinking. This is such bizarre thinking: they expect everyone else to change their way of thinking and go back to the old ways of doing things. Only then will the *-20* seem to be successful. The *-20* lives in the past and longs for everyone else to stay there with them. Since the *-20* has spent their time in the past, once everybody else comes back, the *-20* will be most up to date on the out of date.

How do you feel about the person who was chosen as number three, right behind you?

The *21* thinks in terms of what they could do to help the person behind them. Most of us know the feeling of coming in last or otherwise being an also-ran. We would have appreciated a kind word, some encouragement or, better, some ideas for doing better the next time. *21's* do all they can to help others succeed. They celebrate their wins, but they don't gloat. They accept the praise from others and they usually pass a compliment back to the giver or to someone else who helped them succeed.

The *+20* focuses on how well they did in comparison to the person or people behind them. Almost ignoring the person who is in first place, they focus their words and actions on how much better their accomplishment was than the person they bettered. It's the "I didn't win but I didn't lose" mentality.

The *-20* looks at the person behind them and says, "See, I told you so". *-20's* have spent much of their time and effort trying to convince themselves and others that they cannot win. Seeing someone in the losing position is a confirmation of their opinion.

2. *List your strongest skills and capabilities.*

As you look at your list, answer a couple of questions. First of all, how many of your strongest skills are capabilities you have acquired in the past five years? How many did you develop in the past two years?

21's are continuously updating and upgrading their skills and abilities. It is not uncommon for a ninety-year-old *21* to learn a new language or take up a hobby for the first time. *21's* also know that future success depends on having the skills of the future.

+20's contend that their existing skills are actually improved skills. They are mostly fooling themselves and other *20's*. They bend the rules and definitions enough for their current capabilities to seem advanced or better. As you look at your list, be sure that your current skills are new, not just reworks or enhancements of older ones.

-20's don't see the need for newer skills. They believe that whatever they have learned so far will be sufficient for the future.

To be as objective as possible, ask yourself what you are doing to learn new things. Today we can learn through classrooms, television, books, courses, the internet and through experience. Don't shortchange yourself just because you have not been a classroom or other formal training course in the past two to five years. Certainly continuing education is important, but it can come in many forms.

3. For this question you will need a photograph of yourself from at least five years ago. Looking at the picture and looking in the mirror, answer the following questions.

- ☐ How does the hairstyle compare in the photograph and in the mirror? Worse Same Better
- ☐ How does your style of clothing compare? Worse Same Better
- ☐ How does your physical appearance compare? Worse Same Better

21's are continually improving all aspects of their lives. They are trying to achieve balance in their lives and that means keeping things in perspective as well as keeping things equitable. One area of their life does not move forward while other areas are ignored.

There are some exceptions, of course. **21's** who do not see any value or importance in their appearance will score poorly on this question. However, once it is brought to their attention that they need to improve in this area, they will do what is necessary to improve their appearance.

In general, men are more likely to hang on to older hairstyles and styles of dress than women. Still, either gender will make frequent changes in the way they present themselves if they are **21's**.

+20's will make minor changes in their appearance and refer to it as significant. *-20's* see no reason to change anything about their appearance.

4. List the three goals that are most important to you right now. These are the goals that you focus on virtually every day. If you do not have specific goals, move on to the next question. Once you have written out the goals, answer the following questions.

- ☐ How many of these goals are ongoing goals? Ongoing goals were goals a year ago or several years ago.
- ☐ How many of these goals will require significant change, education or training in order for you to accomplish them?

21's are not afraid to set goals that may require them to learn a little information or even a lot of information. Their percentage of ongoing goals is fairly low. In other words, *21's* set goals, attain them and then move on to the next ones.

+20's set goals that are easy to attain and yet they attain them slowly. There is little challenge in their goals and there are few obstacles to prevent them from attaining them. Still, their goals and dreams seem to drag on for a long time.

-20's do not really set goals. There may be some "Someday I'll..." statements they use that they consider to be goals, but these are usually just to hold up their end of any conversation that might center on goal setting.

5. A person you admire and respect has just achieved some significant success - something you have been trying to accomplish for years. What will you say to them the next time you see them?

6. A person you loathe has just gotten the promotion or position you wanted. What will you say to them the next time you see them?

These two questions focus on a basic human emotion: envy. *21's* are humans and are therefore subject to human frailties. They feel resentment, greed, excitement, loneliness, envy and every other emotion. What makes them different is how they respond to their feelings.

When someone they admire succeeds, they will seek out the other person, congratulate them and begin asking questions. The focus of these questions is for the *21* to learn how to capitalize on what the other person has learned and to use that information to further their own success.

Why would the other person share their ideas? Remember, this is a person that the *21* admires. You can assume then that the other person is also a *21*. *21's* share their knowledge and ideas in the belief that there is no shortage of success and teaching is the best way of learning. Not only are they not threatened by sharing their ideas, they actually benefit from sharing.

When someone that the *21* loathes achieves something the *21* would have liked to accomplish, the *21's* actions are similar even though their purpose is different. The *21* wants to know what he or she is doing wrong or not doing.

For instance, a *21* is up for a promotion. In this case the *21* is an engineer who has submitted many new ideas and modifications that have resulted in new products for the company. The other candidate is a *-20* who has not submitted any new ideas and has, instead, taken pot shots at the ideas the *21* has submitted. The *21* also knows that the *-20* has been saying and doing things to actually subvert the *21's* projects.

The *-20* gets the promotion. The *21* will congratulate the *-20*, just as they would a *21* who had achieved a similar success. However, what the *21* is trying to do is to understand how his or her own actions may have caused the promotion to go to the other person. Was the *21* too aggressive in pushing the ideas forward? Did the new products give more credit to the *21* and not enough to the *21's* boss or others in the department? Did the *21* want the promotion just to show up the *-20*? These are all issues that the *21* will review to help them be more successful next time.

The *+20* will congratulate others who succeed but they do it with gritted teeth and an insincere comment. The *-20's* may pass along an obligatory congratulation but you can be sure they will use every opportunity behind the person's back to cut them down or belittle the accomplishment.

7. The car in front of yours flips over, catches fire and traps the driver inside. You are married and have three small children. Which of the following best describes how you would react:

- ☐ You would attempt a rescue despite the potential danger
- ☐ You would call for professionals to help and in the meantime try to keep others from getting injured
- ☐ You would move out of the way to allow more room for emergency vehicles and personnel

No one really knows how he or she will respond in an emergency or in a stressful situation until they actually face it. On our way to Vietnam, many soldiers boasted of how they would react when they experienced their first trial by fire. The actual reactions for most of them were quite different. Typically, those who talk the most do the least. This is also true in the scenario described in this question.

What this questions actually reveals is how you would like to think you would react. Once under the pressure of the situation, your reaction might be different - it might even surprise you. Still, your thinking determines whether or not you are a *21* and the *21* thinks in terms of doing the right thing regardless of the difficulty.

The *21* thinks in terms of the first response. They are not thinking about the danger, they are focusing on the rescue. This is a significant difference. The *20's* will think only about the potential downside - they might be hurt, their family might suffer, etc. The *21* thinks in terms of a positive outcome. In fact, while attempting the rescue, the *21* will be thinking about the next step: getting the accident victim to the hospital, administering first aid, etc. The *21* assumes a positive outcome from their actions and begins planning for the next step.

The *+20* takes the second approach. Here they are actively involved in calling for help and taking care of others. In their minds at least, they are acting like *21's*. In fact they are making something happen - but what? They are maintaining the status quo. In reality they are doing nothing to improve the situation, only things that will keep the situation from getting worse. Doing things that accomplish nothing is the hallmark of the *+20*.

The *-20* believes that no one can fault them for taking the third approach. After all, they do have a family to consider. They will do all they can to keep from being a hindrance. Let the people who are trained to do the work do it. Don't interfere. In reality, they will be the people on the sidelines who are trying to attribute blame for the accident and who will be criticizing those who attempt a rescue. Being a critical bystander is the hallmark of the *-20* unless, of course, they can actually throw up a roadblock or two. In this case, the *-20* recognizes that hindering a rescue attempt would be frowned upon, so they don't aggressively interfere as they might in other cases.

8. You have reserved your favorite table at your favorite restaurant for a dinner with some of your friends. A person who arrived minutes before you demands "that table" and is seated at your favorite table. Do you...

- ☐ Demand that the manager move the other party
- ☐ Say to the manager, "I see that my favorite table is unavailable, what else do you have?"
- ☐ Leave and vow to never return to that restaurant again

21's make concessions for *20's* and jerks. That is just their way of life. The way this manifests itself is the *21* picks his or her battles. They ask the question, "Is this the hill I want to die on?" There are jerks everywhere and there are many more *20's* than there are *21's*. Winning every battle is a futile and frustrating exercise. Matching wits and battling a *20* for a promotion is a worthwhile endeavor, battling for a table in a restaurant isn't.

21's become proficient in weighing the cost and the benefit of their actions. What if the *21* took on the restaurant manager, the other customer and anyone else they could involve? What would they gain? The meal would begin under tension, harsh words and anger. On the other hand, asking the manager for options opens up some wonderful opportunities. Maybe there is a better table, perhaps the restaurant will provide complimentary desserts - who knows? What an adventure this could turn out to be.

This happened to a client of mine when several of us went to a restaurant he frequented often. The best table was in a corner surrounded by stained glass windows. Or so my client thought. When an arrogant customer demanded the table, my client let the manager off the hook by simply asking what else he had. It turned out that this restaurant has a table in the wine cellar. We were led down some ancient stairs into a wonderful, secluded room surrounded by hundreds, maybe thousands, of bottles of wine. The manager made sure that we had two servers assigned to our table only and he sent platters of every appetizer to the table. It was a great evening.

The *+20* will make a scene, demand their little victory and create a generally unpleasant atmosphere. The *-20* will grumble, never return and have another story to tell about how rotten people are in general.

Things do not always run smoothly for the *21*, any more than they do for the *20's*. In fact, because the *21* is trying to accomplish more and trying to accomplish things that have not been done before, they actually face even more setbacks than the people who are trying to maintain the status quo. Since their minds are usually concentrating on accomplishing big things, there is little time for them to focus on petty battles.

> *9. You and your spouse saved for years to have the cruise you have always wanted. Due to a mechanical malfunction the ship misses a port of call. How do you react?*

The initial reaction for anyone in this situation is one of disappointment and maybe a little anger. That is true for the *20's*

Are You A 21? The Theory of 21 Test

and the *21's*. The difference is that the *21's*, *+20's* and *-20's* will move away from this situation at different speeds.

The *21* will quickly accept that there is nothing that can be done and will begin searching for alternatives. They will ask questions like, what else can we do with this unexpected free time? What are the options available to us? Aren't we always wishing there was more time for certain activities? Well, here is some time, which activity will we explore?

The *+20's* will sit around and complain for whatever amount of time seems appropriate. Once enough people have been made aware of the *+20's* misery and once the *+20* senses that they have milked this one for all it is worth, they will seek some alternative use for the time.

The *-20* will hold on to this terrible mistreatment longer than anyone else could justify. In fact, once they return from their cruise and people ask about their trip, they will begin with, "Well, we missed one port due to mechanical difficulties, and it was the one port we really wanted to see. Poor me, poor me, poor me."

The *21's* may well begin their report with, "The best thing happened. We found ourselves with some unscheduled free time and we were able to...."

Stuff happens. *20's* fall victim to it, *21's* find opportunity in it.

10. List the ten most significant things about your last vacation.

As you review the most significant and memorable things about your last vacation, answer two questions:

1. Are they positive or negative aspects of the trip?
2. Are they significantly different from the things you would have mentioned about your previous vacation?

20's have a tendency to go to the same places and do the same things year after year. This is safe, comfortable and predictable - everything a ***20*** could want in a vacation! Many of their memorable events will be positive and many will be negative, both will have a common theme, however: how did it compare to last time? Positive events will be that the same old restaurant was still there and they served the same old dish and it tasted the same as last time. The hotel still had the same chairs around the pool and the ***20*** could sit in the same place they sat last time. Negative memories will center around things that were not the same such as, "there were too many people - the place has grown too much", or "our favorite restaurant has been remodeled and the food isn't as good". Actually, the food probably hasn't changed but eating it while sitting on different chairs or beside different wallpaper can sure make it taste different to a ***20***.

The list of vacation memories for the ***21*** will include many first time events. A typical list will have entries like, "I tried parasailing and loved it...", "We went snorkeling for the first time and I cannot wait to go again..." There may even be unsuccessful firsts like, "I tried my hand at pottery; I learned I am no potter but I sure had fun..."

Of course we all like doing things so well that we do them repetitively. My wife and I rarely go on any trip near water without packing the snorkeling gear. However, we are constantly seeking new waters and new underwater scenery. We are always on the lookout for new equipment and new techniques that will allow us to enjoy snorkeling even more. Ask us about our last vacations and everyone of them that was near water will mention snorkeling. But every snorkeling adventure we mention was significantly different from the last one. *21's* participate in repetitive activities, but those activities result in different outcomes.

11. Someone is bragging about something they have done (a game of golf they shot, a fish they caught, a major sale they made, etc.). It is obviously an exaggeration. Do you

☐ Nod enthusiastically and congratulate them?

☐ Tell an even better story to hold up your end of the conversation while not making a point of their obvious exaggeration?

☐ Politely express disbelief?

21's have learned that they do not know it all. Things that seem to be utterly impossible to attain are being done daily. The *21* knows that what may seem to be an impossible exaggeration may actually be a fact, a *fait accomplai*. After all, most *21's* have been in the position of having people doubt their accomplishments.

Even if the *21* knows for certain that the person talking has not done what they are professing to have done, they still pass along a compliment and move on. The reason is, the *21* understands that in most cases there is nothing to gain and little to lose in doing so. What difference does it make?

The *+20* is the one who tells the better story. They live with the "That's nothing..." attitude. Whatever your story, they have one better. If you caught a huge fish, they know someone who caught a larger one, a world record. If you shot a great game of golf, they know someone who consistently shoots below par. If you closed a big sale, they know someone who closed a bigger and more difficult sale and whose commission was higher than yours. On it goes.

Do you notice one thing all of the One - Up's have in common? It was someone else who did it. It was a *21* that accomplished something significant and now the *+20* is using that accomplishment to state their position. The *21* was probably someone who the *+20* originally discouraged, about whom the *+20* made disparaging remarks behind their back and to whom the *+20* has said nothing. Interesting, isn't it?

The *-20* challenges anyone's success. It does not even have to be a significant accomplishment, as in this case. It could be a simple win and the *-20* would still challenge the validity or the value of it. After all, success for *-20* is nothing: doing nothing and accomplishing nothing. People who are succeeding make the *-20* look bad so they must take them on and try to make them look bad, or at least worse.

Summary

20's and *21's* differ in their professional lives and in their personal lives. They are different in their thinking, their words and their actions. They differ in their actions and their reactions.

As you may have noticed, some of the questions dealt with things we have done as a result of what we have planned. *20's* live a rote, routine, habitual existence. *21's* seek new adventures and new opportunities. They also think about events that are possible and they plan in advance how they will act and react.

Vince Lombardy once said, "When a prepared man meets opportunity, others call it luck." *21's* aren't lucky; they are prepared. They have spectacular vacations because they seek them out. They

Are You A 21? The Theory of 21 Test

have negative experiences that become positive experiences because they are prepared to seek options.

How many different ways will your actions label you as a ***21*** today?

Chuck Reaves is available for speaking engagements and personal appearances. For more information contact Chuck at:

CHUCK REAVES &
XXI
21 ASSOCIATES

Twenty One Associates Press
P.O. Box 13447
Atlanta, GA 30324
770 979-3321

To order additional copies of this book or to see a complete list of all ADVANTAGE BOOKS™ visit our online bookstore at:

www.advbookstore.com

or call our toll free order number at: 1-888-383-3110

Advantage BOOKS

Longwood, Florida, USA

"we bring dreams to life"™

www.advbooks.com

:d in the United States
'LVS00006B/28-63